WHEN YOU FIND YOURSELF BETWEEN
A ROCK AND A HARD PLACE

CLIMB

THE FAITH TO MOVE MOUNTAINS OFTEN
REQUIRES THE COURAGE TO CLIMB THEM

PAT ROBERTS

CLIMB: The Faith to Move Mountains Often Requires the Courage to Climb Them

Copyright: © 2020 Pat Roberts

All Rights Reserved

Critical Mass Books

ISBN: 978-1-947153-18-9

Cover Design: Eowyn Riggins

Interior Layout: Rachel Greene for elfinpen designs, elfinpen.com

INTRODUCTION
JONATHAN'S WAR

Without faith it is impossible to please God

It is one of the most frank and candid truths in all the Bible. We have heard it a thousand times and quoted it more often than we can remember. It makes for a great wall hanging, meme, or coffee mug inscription. But do we really know what it means? Do we regard it in the sense it was given, or have we removed it so far from its original context that it has become a mere lofty platitude? The powerful phrase is found in the eleventh chapter of the book of Hebrews; a portion of scripture often referred to as the Hall of *Faith*.

It is easy to overlook the unique and poetic writing style of the Apostle Paul. It is no wonder to me why God chose him to write the bulk of the New Testament. What a waste of talent when all he was writing before his conversion were arrest warrants.

His prose is Shakespearean, his insight Orwellian.

"Though I speak with the tongues of men and of angels but have not love, I am nothing."

"And now abides faith, hope, and love, these three; but the greatest of these is love."

"For to me to live is Christ and to die is gain."

"That you may be able to comprehend...the width and length and depth and height of Christ's love."

"Yet in all these things we are more than conquerors through Him who loved us."

"One thing I do, forgetting those things which are behind and reaching forward to those things ahead..."

"Let us run with endurance the race that is set before us."

One of his most captivating treatises is this classic essay on faith in the book of Hebrews. It was an incredibly daunting task to both define and describe the subject of faith and to do it in the past, present and future tense. He begins with historical Jewish examples and then transitions to the great movement of the coming church age. But the greatest challenge in all of this was to make it personal to every believer. The opening line of the monologue is one of the most captivating in all of scripture.

*"Now faith is the assurance of things hoped for, the conviction of things not seen. For by it the people of old **received their commendation**." (ESV)*

It is noteworthy to mention that the myriad people listed in this Hall of Faith were not looking for commendation. Those who seek after a legacy for their own acclaim have missed the point. In fact, I would say that none of those mentioned in this passage were motivated by recognition. They were not looking for fame or a trophy. Quite to the contrary, many did not even want it. Abraham did not want to kill his son, Moses clearly did not want the mantle of leadership, and Daniel did not want to be Little Friskies for the lions. But they all found themselves in a situation **between a rock and a hard place**.

And by faith, they seized the moment and climbed up. Paul said that they no longer even thought about returning to their homeland because their vision was focused on something far better.

The phrase **"by faith"** is used twenty times in this extraordinary passage about ordinary people. Faith was the catalyst that launched the legends of those willing to lead, follow, and die for a cause they hoped for, but had not yet seen. They all died, not having received the promise because other legends were still waiting to be made and there were many more commendations to be handed out.

The apostle goes to great lengths to remind us that faith is actionable. Those who follow God must believe that He openly rewards those who **diligently** seek Him "by faith." But we must be willing to "walk by faith and not by sight" because without faith it is impossible to please Him. It is also why Jesus so often said, "You of little faith." He was not speaking about some type of placid faith. Not the faith that says, "I believe God can do it," but the faith that exclaims, "I believe God can use me to do it."

When hiking the Appalachian Trail, you find it is clearly marked with White and Blue blazes. The white blaze always follows the main trail. The blue will go off trail, sometimes taking you to springs or camp sites. At other times, the blue blaze will take you around the base of the mountain rather than over the mountain. The easier path. The path of faith is never the easier one. Look how Paul phrased it when he spoke about these heroes of faith. They conquered, enforced justice, obtained promises, stopped lions, quenched fire, escaped the sword. How did they accomplish that?

> "They were made strong out of weakness."

Believers today often want God to move mountains because climbing them is too inconvenient. We don't want to climb up, we want someone to throw us a rope or drop us a ladder. These are believers who prefer **accommodation over commendation.** They rely on the faith of others; choosing to use weakness as an excuse rather than an opportunity to be strong. "I'll take the blue blazed path," they exclaim, "and just look at your pictures when you come down."

What is curious to me are the plethora of names not mentioned in this enshrinement. Sure, Paul references that by saying that he could list many more but time had failed him. We can appreciate the need to highlight some of those whose lives and stories were more grandiose and familiar. It is hard to forget Noah and Abraham and Moses and Joseph and David. Even those listed on the undercard like Gideon and Samson and Samuel were fascinating characters. Many are not mentioned by name but rather by exploit, but we can easily match the tale to the character referenced in the story. Examples of these are Elijah, Elisha, Joshua, and Daniel. These stories are epic, ambitious, and larger than life.

Then there are those who fall on the other end of the spectrum. They do not have glorious finales.

The characters lived happily ever after, but not in this world. Their stories are gruesome and their deaths horrific. Without going into specific detail, Paul gives us just enough insight to let our imaginations do the rest. *"Some were tortured, refusing to accept release, so that they might rise again to a better life. Others suffered* *mocking and flogging, and even chains and imprisonment. They were stoned, they were sawn in two, they were killed with the sword. They went about in skins of sheep and goats, destitute, afflicted, mistreated— **of whom the world was not worthy**—wandering about in deserts and mountains, and in dens and caves of the earth."*

There are no names listed in this portion because the number is in the hundreds of thousands. This does not mean that Paul has relegated them to Honorable Mention status. These are not the 'also-ran' members of the team. Quite the opposite. These were the believers who made the ultimate sacrifices knowing full well that their individual acts of courage would contribute to the greater cause. Theirs was the most powerful example of faith. To walk by faith is risky, to live by faith is challenging, to die by faith is the Purple Heart of Christianity. There is no greater love and the world is not worthy of them.

And then there was Jonathan, though he is not mentioned by name. And yet, that is probably the way he would have preferred it. That is how he lived his life. To let his actions speak louder than his words. He avoided the spotlight. Most of his exploits were witnessed by only a few. But they were significant and far reaching. And though we do not find his name recorded in the Hall of Faith, we find his tribute in what he did. It is buried deep in the chapter, at the end of a long paragraph, but just as noteworthy as all the rest: "He ***turned to flight,*** the armies of the aliens."

His story is fascinating and worthy of a deeper look. He sought no legacy or accolade. He placed friendship over blood, loyalty over duty, and yet never compromised on either. In a contemporary world where Christ followers often seek fame and name recognition, where leadership is placed above discipleship, where celebrity is sought more often than humility, Jonathan would never have thrived.

He was an enigma then and now.

His adventure begins between **a rock and a hard place**. It is where he would find himself more than once. That is what makes his life so relevant. It describes where we find ourselves on a great many occasions. Most of the time we are not sure how we arrived there, and even less sure of how we will get out. These dilemmas may involve life decisions, relationships, finances, health, and any number of other stressful situations. We find ourselves trapped between work and family, health and finance, Mastercard and Visa. They are the **occupational hazards** of the world we live in.

At times, however, these circumstances are other-worldly. Our faith will very often place us between a rock and a hard place. It becomes a struggle between God's will and ours, between our world view and His. The skirmish may take place between the confines of flesh and the spirit, Heaven and Hell, or the heart and mind. In the classic novel Moby Dick, this struggle is described in a sermon by Father Maple.

"If we obey God, we must disobey ourselves and it is this disobeying of ourselves where the hardness of obeying God consists."

Faith is the **substance** of things hoped for, the **evidence** of things not seen. (NKJV)

Essentially, faith is about **trust**. It is one of our most powerful and guarded emotions; we give it away very sparingly. We want to trust our friends, our spouse, our authorities, and our media. And whenever this trust is broken, we lose faith. When my daughters were growing up, I cherished their love and respect. But I think more than anything else I wanted them to know they could trust me. Our heavenly Father wants us to believe that we can trust and depend on Him, that He has our best interests at heart. And when we trust Him, it brings Him great pleasure.

You can run from it or at it

One of the most import decisions you will ever make in life is **direction**. At the onset of Jonathan's war, he began to weigh his options, and decided that the only way out was up. The climb would be a struggle and there were no guarantees about what he would find at the top. The word he used to describe it was **'Perhaps.'** But this moment was about faith; he needed to know if his was real and if it had substance and merit. He needed proof, evidence would only be found at the summit. And during his ascent he discovered something vital that every believer must ultimately face.

> The faith to move mountains often requires the courage to climb them

CONTENTS

Introduction: Jonathan's War i

Chapter One: One Day 1

Chapter Two: The Gravity of Faith 19

Chapter Three: UP 35

Chapter Four: Out of the Shadows 55

Chapter Five: Third Tier Leadership 71

Chapter Six: A Rock and a Hard Place 91

Chapter Seven: The Watchmen 111

Epilogue: All Rise 125

For my armor-bearers
My Wife Cindy

This year we celebrate 40 years together. Along our path you have always been my biggest fan, best friend and ardent supporter. You deflect darts and encourage me to keep climbing. Thank you for making the decision to do what I could not; publish this book. With all my love.

My Daughters Jennifer and Jessica

You both inspire me with your compassion and courage through motherhood, teaching, and mission to those less fortunate. Your faith through fostering and adoption reveal an inner strength to raise others UP. You were always the first to launch counterattacks on my behalf. You have my love and admiration.

What is good; and what does the Lord require of you…

…but to do justice, and to love kindness and to walk humbly with your God?

CHAPTER ONE
ONE DAY

"What you get by reaching your destination is not nearly as important as what you will become by reaching your destination." -- Zig Ziglar

War is hell! But only warriors really know what that means. As a history buff, I was always fascinated by the strategies and accounts of war, but they, of course, were always from the critical vantage point of history, never as a participant. You can try to imagine or conceptualize it, but unless you have been in that moment you can never understand it. As a citizen, I have never served in the military. The Viet Nam war ended three months before I graduated from high school; the cold war ensued after that. War has always been part of American history.

Most adults are familiar with the names Valley Forge, Gettysburg, the Alamo, Bunker Hill, and Normandy--battles that turned the tide of war. They are knowledgeable about names like Washington, Grant, Crockett, and Eisenhower. And given the option of multiple choice, they might be able to recognize the dates 1776, 1864, and 1944. But the most important part of history is what we most often forget. The hundreds of thousands of casualties those conflicts created. The insurmountable toll of human life and indescribable bravery of individuals. Many were recipients of the Medal of Honor, the Silver Star, and the Purple Heart. Of all the places I have visited in my life, none was more emotional or contemplative than Arlington Cemetery.

In private surveys taken in recent years, I have discovered from most pollsters, their least favorite subject in high school was History. This is very strange to me because it was one of my favorites. I'm sure the main reason for its lack of popularity was that students didn't see the relevance. It was simply a statistical exercise in names, dates, and places. It most often emphasized the Who-What-When-Where. These are the facts of history, the ones we always had to memorize for tests. For me, the most important part of history is the **Why.** The why creates history and makes the who, what, where, and when relevant today. Visiting old historic towns, battlefields, museums, and antique stores are always reminders to me of how we have arrived at where we are today. We often get lost in the facts of history, but we never forget the Why.

When I turned 50 someone gave me a birthday card filled with facts about 1955, the year I was born.

It included interesting items about cost of living prices, sports and music. It also listed the names of famous people who were born that same year, Bill Gates, Steve Jobs, Kevin Costner, and Whoopi Goldberg. What was curious to me was the absence of what was possibly the most consequential story of the year, the story of a young black woman who refused to give up her bus seat. On the occasions when I teach history, it never begins with the time or location. We make our way back to that, but the conversation always originates with the "Why."

Through the years there have been various accounts of what happened on the bus that day. But when asked directly, this is what Rosa Parks said. "People always say that I didn't give up my seat because I was tired, but that isn't true. I was not tired physically…No, the only tired I was, was tired of giving in."

The Why tells the story; the facts are simply answers on history tests and trivia games. The why changes history. A war, whether international, civil, or personal, is always a war about ideology, humanity, and conviction. A seat on bus began with one person but started a movement which changed a country and an individual who was later honored with the Presidential Medal of Freedom.

What inspires valiant people?

Each of us is fighting our own private wars. The conflicts may be small skirmishes or all-out assaults. Sometimes we contract mercenaries or mediators or counsellors, but sooner or later we must decide what it is we are willing to live and die for. Where will the courage come from? Often, it is a cause or a creed that someone believes in deeply. At other times it is determined by the situation that they are thrust into. And then there are those moments when we are just tired, weary of being pushed down, exhausted from apathy and too fatigued to be afraid anymore. During these instants, people are not necessarily attempting to change the course of history, merely refusing to accept their current circumstances. They are not ready to give up; they are just tired of giving in. Feeling like life is closing in from both sides, they find themselves **between a rock and a hard place**. And though they are overwhelmed, anxious, and uncertain, they somehow find the strength to climb. An ordinary day becomes an extraordinary moment. And it is in those moments when something dramatic takes place; when lives are changed, and a new direction is forged. That direction is always **Up.**

I Samuel 14--One Day

There once was an army on the precipice of defeat. They were hiding in rocks and caves and pits. Their forces were disjointed, isolated, and discouraged. The commander seemed at a loss for strategy and a path forward. There seemed to be no tactical solutions, no way to advance from a military perspective. For the enemy, it was a conquest for dominance. For this army it was a battle for existence and a struggle for survival. And then, **"one day"** became the turning point in the war.

"Get up!"

The soldier on the ground felt the foot nudging him mildly in the back but exhaustion kept him from even rolling over. The second kick was more attention grabbing.

"Get up, we're moving out!"

"Who ordered that?" he asked, as he rubbed his eyes.

"I did," replied the captain.

As the corporal rose, he realized that no one else seemed to be moving.

With a puzzled look he enquired, "What are we doing?"

"We are going to do some recon. Get your gear, and do it quietly."

The corporal was a weapons expert. He was not only knowledgeable in warfare, he was young and strong, capable of hiking and packing heavy amounts of armor. But his orders today were different.

"Just your sword and my bow." *Okay*, he thought. *Traveling light means we aren't planning to do anything foolish. Just a day of gathering intel.*

The captain's name was Jonathan; he was the general's son. Their relationship was best described as tenuous. As a son he had great respect for his father; as a soldier he often questioned the decisions of his commander and chief. In this instance, the decision to take matters into his own hands was his alone. "It's easier to ask forgiveness than permission," is how the adage goes. Though Jonathan knew that forgiveness was probably not going to be an option. He wasn't being foolhardy; he was simply leading in the only way he knew how—from the shadows.

The first step was crossing through the demilitarized zone. Not much harm in this, so long as no one took any threatening action. The opposing army were ensconced on the high ground, always a must in any military campaign. Vantage point does just that--gives you the advantage. Up is always best; but it is never easy taking the hill. Still, that wasn't what this mission was, at least not yet. This was just about walking through the safe zone, gathering information, and weighing options. Nothing drastic.

As the two-man advance team moved past the DMZ, they entered a large ravine. The pass would not be easy. To the north was an escarpment of stone and rocks nearly 1500 feet high. Scaling that wall would be a challenging task even for an expert climber. The slope on the south was not much better. It was a crag of boulders and sediment that rose vertically to the peak. It was hard to say how high it was, but it was high enough. These cliffs were named Bozez (shining) and Seneh (thorn) and were infamously known as being impassable. And so, these two war-weary soldiers found themselves between...

a Rock and a Hard Place.

"Maybe we should just take the intel we've gathered and go report to the general?"

For a moment, the captain did not answer. Why should he? He just needed to give the order. But again, that is not who he was. He had put this soldier's life on the line and felt like he was entitled to know the truth.

"Because the general doesn't even know we are here!"

The pause was long and silent. After a few moments, the corporal started to speak but then held his tongue. A few seconds later his mouth moved but no words came out. After giving some thought to the situation he decided that maybe some clarification was in order.

"Does anyone know we are here?"

"No," Jonathan replied.

Again, another long pause.

"Do you at least have a plan?"

"Not really," said Jonathan. "I'm just kind of making this up as I go."

"Okay," the corporal answered, wishing now that he had enlisted in the Navy instead of the Marines. "Let me hear what you have so far."

"Alright. Here is what I am thinking. First, we break cover and show ourselves to the enemy. Then, if they tell us to come up to them, we climb up this cliff and attack."

"That's it?" asked his companion. "That's all you've got?"

"Well, I didn't say it was a great plan," admitted the captain.

Then the corporal responded. "So, let me ask you this. How many do you think there are?"

"Not sure," was the comeback. "It's a garrison, so I'm guessing around 20."

"You're guessing?"

Jonathan thought for a moment and then said, "No. You're right. You should head back and report."

"Wait," he responded. "So, we are outnumbered twenty to two?"

"Well, that's one way to look at it," said Jonathan.

"What is another way?" came the quick retort.

"I believe deeply that God is with us. And if he chooses, He can save our people with a great army or with just a few good men."

The corporal realized in that moment there was something much deeper driving his captain. This was not merely another mindless military maneuver to take a hill. There was something at stake much greater than his own life. He needed to know if his faith was real. The victory wasn't impossible for God, but it would only be made possible through faith. There was no other way to find His favor.

"Do you think God will fight with us?" asked the corporal.

"Perhaps" was all Jonathan could offer.

"PERHAPS!!! That...that's all you've got? Not even a probably, just a possibly?"

"This is what I know," said Jonathan, "I would rather climb up and die on that mountaintop than crawl back down and hide in a hole."

The corporal thought deeply for a moment about those alternatives. His captain was not giving him a direct order to climb up after him. He wanted instead for this soldier to come to the realization about what was at stake. For his eyes to be open about the greater good. He looked back down through the ravine; then he looked up to the precipice that was before him.

"Twenty to two, huh? I like those odds. I'm in!" he exclaimed.

"Before we enter this foray," said his captain, "I need to know you are in all the way."

"Heart and Soul," was his reply.

"Alright, then," said Jonathan, **"let's climb!"**

They say the bond between a band of brothers in war is as strong as any family bond. But in this case it was even more than that. It was not that this soldier simply believed in his captain. It was that he believed in the faith of his captain. Jonathan was so committed to the cause that he raised others UP around him. Faith has the power to elevate all those who are in contact with it.

Endless possibilities, but no guarantees

Perhaps might be the very best word to describe faith. It is the unknown and uncertain that causes our anxiety. We believe in God; we believe that nothing is impossible for God, and we believe that we can do all things through Christ's strength. We believe--until we are asked to prove it. We believe until that moment our faith is put to the test. Do not confuse "perhaps" with doubt. Doubt is the fear that either God or we do not have the ability. Jonathan knew God could, he just wasn't sure He would. And so, he did what we all do at times: we ask for a sign, a clear signal or confirmation of some kind that what we are about to do, by faith, is what God is leading us to do. Jonathan made no promise or proclamation of victory. He simply said that this was the direction that God was leading. He wasn't positive God would do something amazing, but he wanted to be there if He did.

If our parents ever said "Maybe," we knew the answer was "NO!" Let me think about it, we'll see, let me ask your father/mother, et cetera. It's not hard to understand why people do the same thing when they grow up, not only to their children but in almost every decision. And when Jesus pushed the envelope by saying, "Let your yes be yes and your no be no," most often, people said no.

Jonathan has always been my favorite Bible personality. He was loyal, dependable, humble, unassuming, courageous, and honorable. Most of what he is remembered for was done behind the scenes with few or no witnesses. His conflicts dealt more with relationships than armies. He was a bold and seasoned warrior, but it was the private skirmishes that were waged in closed rooms and empty fields that revealed his greatest courage. The inner turmoil and anguish between people he loved were the battlefields where he spent most of his time. And during most of those wars he served as a mediator between the king who was and the king who was to be.

An incredibly deep faith in God and personal awareness in himself drove the choices and decisions that led to his greatest victory and ultimately to his untimely death. Love of country, honor among family, and loyalty to friends were the hallmarks of his life. And through it all he knew exactly who he was, and he was content with that. He was uncommonly comfortable outside of the spotlight. There are many in leadership who do not understand that type of personality and attitude, especially those who lean toward narcissistic behavior. Jonathan did not aspire to leadership, at least, in the sense that it is usually defined today. But he was always bold to speak his mind and hold to his conviction, which never goes well with narcissistic leaders.

Sadly, his own father, Saul, would fall into that trap. He would walk away from God's agenda and set his own. And as the very first king of Israel, he would set a standard for all who followed. It would become the basis for what separated good kings from evil ones, what distinguished the humble from the arrogant. In an effort to build their own name recognition they forgot what the original purpose was. That is why there were always prophets, to remind the leaders of what that purpose was: not for them to be remembered, but to lead the people to remember who God is. To live by faith in Him. One of the most memorable examples of this was between a king named Jehoiakim (also known as Shallum) and the prophet Jeremiah.

To truly know God

King Jehoiakim, you are doomed! You built a palace with large rooms upstairs. You put in big windows

and used cedar paneling and red paint. But you were unfair and forced the builders to work without pay. More cedar in your palace doesn't make you a better king than your father Josiah. He always did right—he gave justice to the poor and was honest. That is what it means to truly know God. Jeremiah 22

Faith is not belief in the existence of God. The devil believes in God. It is not having a knowledge of who God is. Faith is simply a lifestyle of pursuing the path that God has laid out for humanity as a whole and for our own individual race that we run. Faith is to know God's heart and follow his agenda. That is to defend truth and to defend those who cannot defend themselves. It is about integrity and courage. Those two things defined Jonathan.

Shelter in Place

While writing the first chapter of this book I heard a brief news item about a virus near Wuhan, China, that they were calling Corona. At that time, it was just a footnote on television. By the time I got to chapter two we were closing borders and bringing in medical experts. Halfway through chapter three we were in total lockdown and told to "shelter in place." This plan was going to be our best hope to save thousands of lives. It was during the next thirty days of the pandemic, while working on the next couple of chapters, it occurred to me that this is exactly what Jonathan and his army had been doing. As I continue to write, many states, including mine, are beginning to open **UP** the economy. There is no small shortage to the debate and strategy to accomplish this next step of moving forward. Many believe we should wait for an antidote or vaccine. Others believe that waiting for a cure will be worse than the disease. Jonathan was sheltered in place, and he realized it was time to go out and to go UP.

The Why

During our current crisis, that has been a question that has risen to the forefront. Eventually we will be seeking answers to the how-when-where of the Covid-19 virus. My guess is that Jonathan and the Israelites were also asking God, "Why?" If they were His chosen, then why were they losing to their mortal enemy? Again, the why changes history. When people ask, "Why do bad things happen?" it is not really the answer that will make the difference. It is the choice of what we do next that determines the future. When his brothers cowered, Jonathan chose to climb. He was not positive that the answer was Up there, but he knew it was not Down here. Hardship is a difficult struggle, and heartache exponentially amplifies the challenge. The past and its pain are like hiking with a 100 lb. backpack.

But we are not the only ones who ask Why. It is a question that God asks about us, as well. He always knows the Who-What-When-Where to every inquiry. And yet, there remain certain things about our faith that still seem to puzzle Him. Jesus asked his followers often, "Why did you doubt?" "Why do you worry?" "You have ears, why can you not hear?" "Why could you not stay awake and pray?" "Why do you always seek a sign?" The confusion is a two-way street and both sides are often puzzled as to the other's motivation. We sometimes believe that God takes an ad hoc approach to our life and He is frequently baffled by our guttural response to every difficult situation.

There is nothing wrong with the Why question. The reason we ask is because we love, because we care.

The sociopath will never ask why. There is no reason or logic that will satisfy them. It is when we stop asking why that we should be afraid. That is like the white flag of surrender. The why should not be the stopping point, it should be the starting line. The question should be motivational not debilitating. Being inquisitive lets us know we are alive. Life is often like a lengthy algebraic equation. It takes a long time to solve it and even when we arrive at the correct answer, most of us still do not understand its purpose.

Some describe Christianity as a race, a journey, a path, a walk, a climb. In truth, it is all those things. The real challenge is being able to discern one from the other. How do we distinguish between the times when we are to run and the times we are supposed to walk? When do we listen and when do we act? At what points do we stop and learn and at what moments do we teach? The journey is filled with both excitement and angst.

Solomon said that there is a time and season for everything under the sun. Sometimes we plant, sometimes we reap. At times we weep and at times we laugh; there are moments when we mourn and others when we dance. There are times when we should speak and others when we should be silent. There are periods when we gather and others when we should cast away. There are times we are to love as well as things we are to hate. There is a time of war and a time of peace. That is the place where Jonathan currently found himself. He knew it was a time to climb because there was no other choice. He could no longer sit and ponder, and he could not run. Peace talks had ended, there was nothing left to learn. This was not a time to write in his journal or record his memoirs. This was a moment to do something bold.

I Samuel 14--*One day*

Jonathan the son of Saul said to the young man who carried his armor, "Come, let us go over to the Philistine garrison on the other side." But he did not tell his father. Saul was staying in the outskirts of Gibeah in the pomegranate cave at Migron. And the people did not know that Jonathan had gone.

Within the passes, by which Jonathan sought to go over to the Philistine garrison, there was

a rocky crag on the one side and a rocky crag on the other side. *The name of the one was Bozez, and the name of the other Seneh. The one crag rose on the north in front of Michmash, and the other on the south in front of Geba. Jonathan said to the young man who carried his armor, "Come, let us go over to the garrison of these uncircumcised. It may be that the Lord will work for us, for nothing can hinder the Lord from saving by many or by few." And his* *armor-bearer said to him, "Do all that is in your heart. Do as you wish. Behold, I am with you heart and soul." (ESV)*

CHAPTER TWO
THE GRAVITY OF FAITH

"Faith is the heroic effort of your life; you fling yourself in reckless confidence toward God."
-- Oswald Chambers

It has been said that altitude is affected by attitude; but I don't think we should easily dismiss fear from the equation. Acrophobia is both a mental and spiritual condition. Faith is a thrill ride, a roller coaster experience. There will be lots of laughs, lots of screams, and lots of twists and turns. Amusement parks add to the terror by naming these scream machines—The Beast, Mindbender, Super Duper Looper, Exterminator, Prime-evil,

Intimidator, Fury, Wicked, and Apocalypse. By faith, we climb aboard these terrifying attractions—Doubt, Worry, Fear, Uncertainty, and Discomfort. We strap in and hold on!

The most difficult aspect of hiking and rock climbing is **gravity**. Even if you can get past your paranoia of heights and fear of falling, there remains **the climb**. The resistance, sweat, body aches, and mental fatigue all take their toll. And you are not sure which discomfort is most unpleasant, the chest pain in your lungs or the cramps in your legs. The descent is challenging, to be sure. But the one obstacle you do not have to overcome on the way down is gravity. That is only common to the ascent.

Life is not measured in years or accomplishments or distance. It is measured mostly by **topography**.

Let me explain. The Appalachian Trail is 2,180 miles long running from Georgia to Maine. Over the past twenty years I have hiked approximately 600 miles of it in ten different states. It is unlikely that I will ever complete all of it, but I look forward to hiking in the three or four states that remain and maybe getting to at least the 1,000-mile mark. That number, however, is insignificant compared to what the experience has been.

Topography basically refers to ascent and descent. Every hike on the Trail is grouped into one of three categories: easy, moderate, and strenuous. At times you walk up and at times you walk down. But do not be deceived; downhill can be some of the most dangerous. It is much easier to fall going down than up. Often this is because we become careless and lackadaisical. The ascent takes more determination. The resistance takes its toll on lungs and muscle as well as mind. It is like aerobic exercise.

Before every hike, I always check the topo-map. This is important to me because I want to know what I might see and experience that day. Is there a waterfall, a summit view, wildlife, a historic location? Hiking to me is not about how far and fast I can travel in a day; it is about what I want to remember about that day. Several years ago, I hiked in West Virginia downhill to Harper's Ferry. The next morning, I got up very early, crossed the state line and ascended to the Maryland Heights Overlook. From there you view the merging of the Potomac and Shenandoah Rivers and I wanted to witness it at sunrise. What I wanted to experience on the Trail that day was dictated by topography.

Life and faith are both like that. I am again reminded by what Jesus said, that real life is not the accumulation of possessions, but rather the accumulation of experiences and the joy of deep and meaningful relationships. If we prepare well for the walk, and discipline our self, we will love where the path takes us, enjoy the memories, and grow from the experience.

The **Gravity of Christianity** is that its most critical tenets are action oriented. Prayer and love and faith are not concepts which we adorn, they are convictions lived out. To "walk by faith" is not a stroll through a dewy meadow.

It is often a path through a dark valley or atop a stormy sea. It leads us to places and circumstances with clear purpose but with outcomes that are not always apparent or certain. Like rock climbing, it is often just grabbing on to the next point in front of you. But it is not freestyle climbing—you are always attached to the vine and anchored to the rock. However, reaching the top takes incredible amounts of **stamina**. Even in the training and preparation, before we begin the ascent, we are given careful instruction. You will need to be patient in affliction. At times you will have to endure hardship. There will be storms and obstacles you did not anticipate, but do not look back or look down. **Commit to the climb**. Even if, at times, it is on your hands and feet.

To be fair there is no real dignity in this type of climbing. Several years ago, I had the opportunity to hike with a friend who lived near the Sonoma Mountains just outside of Tucson, AZ. She had hiked to the summit before, but from the "touristy" side of the trail. Since I was an experienced hiker, she decided that we would access the path from the backcountry. This involved a two-mile trek through the desert, which was beautiful in the early morning hours. She failed to let me know that it would be 95 degrees on the way back. The trail was rocky and formidable. At times it would end at a rock face and we would scale 20 feet to find the path again. At times I was not sure we were even still on the path. There were places where we climbed over boulders on our hands and feet. It was often not pretty. At one moment I slipped in the pea gravel, fell into some cactus, and spent the next 15 minutes picking barbs out of my hand. What made matters worse was being passed by a 72 year old woman with her two great grandchildren who asked, "Grandma, is that man okay?"

It's at these moments your mind begins to play tricks on you. Is reaching the peak worth all of this? Can I even make it? Is my life insurance up to date? But as always, the summit is worth the climb. The 360- degree panoramic views were incredible. We took a long time to rest, eat lunch, talk about life, and take dozens of pictures. We were a third of the way down when I realized that I had left my phone/camera at the top. I had to go back because it was the only proof that I had made it. On the hike back up, all I could think about was, "Where is that grandma when I need her?"

Gravity

"So, what is our next move?" asked the corporal.

"We are going to let them know we are here," came the response.

"Okay, let's call that Plan B," said the weapons carrier.

The corporal was not a great military mind. That is why he was an armor bearer and not a general. But he did know that one of the last things you do in battle is give away your position.

"I was thinking more along the lines of a covert operation. Maybe we can use stealth to our advantage."

"No! We are going to do just the opposite; we are going to make a lot of noise," said Jonathan.

"Are you sure? I mean, I'm just thinking out loud here, but maybe we could sneak up on them."

"Nope," said the captain. "Desperate times call for desperate measures! We are going to reveal ourselves. If they say, 'Wait there, we are coming down to you,' then we get ready. But if they say, 'Come up here,' then we **go up**."

The first thing that entered the corporal's mind was the hope that they would come down and surrender. *Of course not*, he thought. *Why would they come down? That would be too easy.*

"Come up here," said the enemy, "and we will show you a thing or two!"

The corporal looked down, gently sighed, and then looked back at his captain.

"Somehow I knew that would be their response," he said.

But Jonathan replied, "That's our sign! Let's move out. I'll go first, you follow me up."

Oh great, he thought. "I get to die second," he mumbled under his breath.

"Look, the cowards are coming out of the holes where they have been hiding!" said the garrison.

Then Jonathan **CLIMBED UP** on his **hands and feet**, and his armor-bearer after him.

The Philistines were the mortal enemy of Israel. They were the Nazis of the Old Testament. They did not just want to dominate the Jews, they wanted to exterminate them. Philistines were the most brash, smack-talking bullies of the day, using fear and intimidation as their strongest weapon. They were braggarts and bullies. And like Hitler, their downfall was their arrogance. These two soldiers were about to call their bluff. It wouldn't be the last time that this would happen, but it would be the first. What came next, they never expected; to say it caught them off guard would be drastically understated.

And in that first strike, Jonathan and his armor bearer killed about 20 men, maybe a couple less or more.

Now you may be thinking, "Well that's pretty impressive, but nothing compared to some of the epic skirmishes we read about in other Biblical accounts." Remember, however, this was before the battle between David and Goliath. At that point, no one even knew who David or Goliath was. This was long before Saul had killed his thousands and David his ten-thousands. It was decades after the exploits of Samson and years before the marvels of David's mighty men. At this moment in history, Jonathan was a trailblazer. He didn't kill his thousands; he only took out twenty. But he set the precedent. Not as a prototype for war, but as a statement of faith.

When I was young, Saturday morning television was about heroes, and we had a lot to choose from. When everything seemed hopeless and there was nowhere to turn, we would hear these classic lines.

"Look, up in the sky! It's a bird, it's a plane, no, it's Superman."

"Hi-Ho Silver!" The Lone Ranger riding on a white steed to the William Tell overture meant all was well. A small rodent named Mighty Mouse always assured us, "Here I come to save the day"!

And then there was Popeye. The pipe-smoking, tattooed sailor who cursed under his breath. He was the first anti-hero, remembered mostly for his iconic self-awareness: "I yam's what I yam's." He didn't fight against super villains or have superpowers. But he did stand up to bullies. He fought for the honor of women. He taught us the importance of eating our veggies. But his most heroic act is one that most people do not remember. It was his role as a father to his "adopted" son, Sweet Pea. Someone had left the baby on Popeye's doorstep and he assumed the responsibility to raise him as his own. He never saved the world, but he loved and protected his family.

There was one other Saturday morning hero who might have had the most memorable line of all. "There's no need to fear, Underdog is here." It was the anthropomorphic canine with a cape, squeaky voice, and biceps the size of golf balls. To look at him was to think, "There is good reason to fear."

I'd rather have the little rat or the guy with the spinach.

Nothing in sports does more to bring excitement and suspense to a game than the **underdog**. Especially if you have "no dog in the fight." The one most likely to win is called the favorite but, more often, the favorite of the spectator is the underdog. What creates the suspense is he Chance. Jonathan knew he was the underdog; that is why he said, "*Perhaps* the Lord will give us the victory." But he was also confident in the enemy's over-confidence. That is usually what happens when underdogs win. It is how David later defeated Goliath. And it was why, years later, his son, Solomon, would write...

"The race is not always to the swift or the battle to the strong, but time and chance happen to them all."

Faith is the "substance" of things hoped for. In our modern vernacular we would call it **the stuff**. It is the stuff we are hoping for, the results. But they are not guaranteed. If they were, it would not be faith. We must also remember that the outcome may not be the way we envisioned it. One skirmish may only be a part of the greater good. To win a war, you'll probably lose a few battles.

The odds of Jonathan winning were at the least 20-1, but he beat the oddsmakers. Jonathan didn't know what God was going to do, he only knew what he had to do. He wasn't planning on saving the day, but he wanted to be there if God did. Jonathan was the first, but his name became legendary. After that, everyone wanted to name their son John. It became one of the most common names in scripture and in history. But only because of faith. If he had 20 men and there was only one enemy, we wouldn't remember his name.

Years later the armor-bearer recounts the story, either to Samuel or possibly to the prophet Nathan. There was no embellishment, accolade, or self-glory. We never even know his name. "I just carried his bow," he probably said. His account begins with the what, where, when, and how of the events that day. But then he moves to the Why. Why did Jonathan do it? Because he was tired. Not physically, just tired of giving in. Tired of being stuck between a rock and a hard place. Ready to climb.

I can envision the story making its way from house to house and throughout the country. In another province a young boy hears the tale of how Jonathan saved the day. It inspires his own faith in God. So much so that even as a small shepherd he would find courage to protect his flock, even from lions and bears. Jonathan became his hero and though he did not know it then, he would later become his best friend. Young David would soon be called upon to follow his own path that God had set before him. A journey that would begin with his first job in the military--to serve as King Saul's armor-bearer.

When David prepared for his fight with Goliath, he took five stones from the river. Some believe this was because the giant had four brothers. I have a little different take. David was confident in his skill, but to just bring one stone would be arrogant. Faith requires trust, but it also entails wisdom. Scripture mandates that we walk in both. Being bold does not mean being foolish.

Risk Management

We often hear the terms Blind Faith and Leap of Faith. The problem is that neither of those accurately describe faith. Blind is not good. Jesus spent a great deal of time healing the blind and warning us not to let the blind lead the blind or they will both fall off the cliff. Climbing is hard; jumping is foolish. That is why the Bible says, "By faith." We are told to "walk by faith" but also to "walk as wise." In other words, be bold but not foolish. **Faith is when God tests our limits; foolish is when we test His**.

This is what we tend to do. We climb to the top and peer over. We begin to make assessments. Hmmm! Twenty to one. So, we begin to calculate. We factor in risk/reward. We do the math of diminishing return. Is this mountain even worth taking? Or worse, we try to find every excuse not to take the risk. We come down and make a report. "There is one old man, he is in a wheelchair, with a therapy dog, and a BB gun." Wow, that BB gun sounds like it could be trouble. **Perhaps**, if he didn't have that gun. Risk management isn't about avoiding the risk. The point Jonathan was making when he decided to show himself to the enemy, was that he knew he would then be committed. I'm sure his armor-bearer thought, "So, what if we kill the twenty. What then?" That's where faith comes in.

Jonathan's decision was to commit to what he could do; what happened after that would be in God's hands. Faith is the substance of things we hope for, the conviction that God can provide them.

Our enemy is referred to as "a roaring lion." That is his strategy: to make a lot of noise in hopes that we will be terrified. It is what bullies do. But we would do well to remember that there were four times in the Bible that people faced lions—David, Benaiah, Samson, and Daniel. And the lions lost every time; they were 0-4. Who were these...Detroit Lions? The devil does not want you to live by faith; he wants you to walk in fear. I do not remember who said it or where I read it, but I have never forgotten it.

Fear never moves out on its own, it must be evicted

Too many believers simply attempt to **manage life** between the rock and the hard place.

"It is what it is." Really? Or is that just an excuse to make no effort? To become a victim or martyr.

It amazes me how so many people choose to live such a banal existence. They have no challenges, are making no difference, and are content with this sedentary life. People live on auto pilot, vaguely dissatisfied and disinterested.

Their lives have become a yawn. When was the last time you had an experience so incredible it was hard to describe in words? People don't aspire anymore. Forget climbing up, they do not even look up! Watch the people around you. Our entire society is in a constant state of looking down. Frozen to a little screen watching other people live their lives.

Paul admonished us to "Live a life worthy of your calling." God is the choreographer of our life. He composes the sequence of steps and moves for our performance. He lays out the steps and if we trust him, He will guide us along the path. Maybe your climb is a new direction, change of attitude, change of lifestyle. Or maybe it is not about you at all. In fact, the opposite is probably true. The climb is about using your faith to change the course of others. Jesus said He had come to give sight to the blind, heal the sick, and set the captives free. Nothing in that was about Him.

Believers tend to be extremely reticent about their faith. They try to be very discreet with others because they believe that faith is only between them and God, therefore, they do not readily reveal it. But to God, faith should be an open book. He is ready to pour blessings and accolade on our endeavors, to assign recognition for work well done. Not for our fame, but for the notoriety of what this kind of love can accomplish in the world, through faith. Paul wrote that this kind of love should be without dissimulation. This means that it is not disguised or concealed. He said that our love should be genuine

(Romans 12), that true love does not seek its own (1 Corinthians 13), and that we should do nothing out of selfish ambition, but in sincerity prefer others above ourselves (Philippians 2). Love is authentic, not like the Pharisees who flaunted their religion. Jesus said they have their reward, but it was temporary and extraneous. There is laid up for us a crown of righteousness.

Jonathan was not making that climb for himself or for fame. He was fighting for his brothers, for his country, and for a faith that he wanted to prove was real. He was climbing for an ideology that he had believed in all his life. This belief taught that God would reward him for his action and hold him culpable for his inaction. He was fighting for a God who had promised that He would fight for him. He was climbing because that is what was required.

What Does the Lord Require? Micah 6 (ESV)

"With what shall I come before the Lord, and bow myself before God on high? Shall I come before him with burnt offerings, with calves a year old? Will the Lord be pleased with thousands of rams, with ten thousands of rivers of oil? Shall I give my firstborn for my transgression, the fruit of my body for the sin of my soul?" He has told you, O man, what is good; and what does the Lord require of you...

...but to do justice, and to love kindness, and to walk humbly with your God?

> Gravity is both our greatest enemy
> and strongest ally.

The reason is because this will not be our only climb. There is not just one mountain in our life. Faith is a mountain range and by conquering each hilltop we grow stronger for the next. Don't ever give up or give in! Don't ever stop climbing or fighting with every breath here on earth. God has you here for a specific purpose and wants you to complete it. He uses real people in the hard places of real life to work out His plan, often sown in tears, struggle, and failure. Sometimes we stall and God will allow circumstances to happen that force us to move; trust the transition. If we finish the course, the result is unimaginable.

"He who chooses the beginning of a road chooses the path where it leads". --Harry Emerson Fosdick

I Samuel 14—The Climb

Then Jonathan said, "We will cross over to the men, and we will show ourselves to them. If they say to us, 'Wait until we come to you,' then we will stand still in our place, and we will not go up to them. But if they say, 'Come up to us,' then we will go up, for the Lord has given them into our hand. This will be the sign to us." So, both men showed themselves to the garrison of the Philistines. And the Philistines said, "Look, Hebrews are coming out of the holes where they have hidden themselves." And the men of the garrison hailed Jonathan and his armor-bearer and said, "Come up to us, and we will show you a thing." Jonathan said to his armor-bearer, "Come up after me, the Lord has given them into the hand of Israel."

*Then Jonathan CLIMBED UP on his hands and feet, and his armor-bearer after him. And they fell before Jonathan, and his armor-bearer killed them after him. And that first strike, which Jonathan and his armor-bearer made, killed about twenty men within as it were half a furrow's length in an acre of land. And there was a panic in the camp, in the field, and among all the people. The garrison and even the raiders trembled, the earth quaked, and it became **a very great panic.***

CHAPTER THREE
UP

"Set your minds on things that are above...not on things that are on the earth." –Paul the Apostle

"Get up!" Every morning began the same way. The comfortable confines underneath a warm, cozy blanket. The innocent carefree dreams of youth, running through the woods or swimming in the lake. Then, the still of the night shattered by the voice of the woman who supposedly loved her child. "Wake up; it's time to get up!" She had done the same thing to me after only nine months in the womb. "It's time to get out!" Why? I'm quite content here. It was always confusing as a child to think about starting the day when it was still dark. I didn't understand much about the world, but I knew the difference between day and night, and the dark was for sleeping. As a child there was little I dreaded more than getting up.

As an adult I have always been a morning person with a deep affection for being up early. The calm and peace of pre-dawn have an appeal to me that many do not relate to. In a day that is destined for noise and possible chaos, early morning provides a place of solitude and quiet that I may not see for the rest of the day. Watching the sun rise is a creative marvel that never grows old. Observing the light overcome the darkness is a magnificent source of inspiration. Early is my prime time. Often, more meaningful things are accomplished for me in the first three hours than in the rest of the day.

Night people will never comprehend this even though nature reveals it every day. The sun goes *down*. That means it is time to slow down not speed up. It is the time when my phone blows up with texts, emails, and social media frenzy. Of all the marvels of modern technology, the greatest achievement on a smart phone is the silence button. Morning is for getting up; nighttime is for shutting up. Yes, I realize that I am in the silent majority on this issue, but I rather enjoy being a part of the majority that is silent.

Now, it must be noted that being up early is not the same thing as getting up early. Getting up is not always an easy task, but it is the price that must be paid for being up. One thing that always helps motivate me is COFFEE! In fact, UP is where we all aspire to and yet it is never the path of least resistance. Ascending to the mountaintop involves gravity, sweat, and endurance. But it is always a better direction than the alternative. Down is easier, but less rewarding.

Upward Mobility

The Bible is littered with pleas to live in "up mode." We are implored to rise up, lift up, look up, build up, gather up, and store up. Those who found themselves in desperate situations responded:

Jonathan—when he was at the doorstep of defeat—Climbed Up

Abraham—when directed by God--Offered Up

Joshua—when assisting Moses in battle--Lifted Up

Elijah—when he heard a still small voice--Rose up

Jairus' daughter—when raised from the dead--Sat Up

The Prodigal—when he came to his senses—Got Up

It may be why the Psalmist often asked, "Why so downcast, O my soul? Why so disturbed within? Put your hope in God."

Timeless Tales

Scripture is filled with personal accounts of real people who found themselves between a rock and a hard place, struggling under great duress between their faith and their future. Knowing that they couldn't go back but not seeing a clear path of direction ahead. Followers of God leading altruistic lives only to see their hopes and dreams shattered. In some cases, the future looked dim, in others completely dark.

These are not the only moments when we experience faith, but they are the occasions when it is put to its greatest test.

A "Handmaid's Tale" (Genesis 21)

It is one of those scandalous accounts that many seem to simply gloss over. A true "hand-maid's tale" of upper and lower class citizens. Hagar and her son Ismael had become victims of social out-casting, sent into the desert with nothing but a small canteen of water. With no resources and little hope of survival, the story speaks to the darkness in the creature and to the grace of the Creator. When all seems lost, we often need someone to shout these words to us. **"Up! Get up!"** God made a promise, and as we learn in scripture, He is never slack in keeping them. He said to Hagar "I will make your son into a great nation." But what he needed her to do in that moment was to "Get up!"

And so, **he opened her eyes** and she saw a pool of water. (vs. 19)

Surrounded (2 Kings 6)

It was early one morning when the servant of Elisha rose and went out. What he observed sent sheer horror through his veins. An alien army with horses and chariots had surrounded the city. He fell to his knees and screamed out to his master, "What shall we do?" Elisha was calm and collected. "Do not be afraid, for those who are with us are more than those who are with them." I can envision Elisha telling his servant to have faith and to get up.

So, the Lord **opened the eyes** of the young man and behold, the mountain was full of horses and chariots of fire all around Elisha. (vs. 17)

A Walk in the Clouds (Luke 24)

Three days had passed since the brutal death of their leader. Two of His disciples were walking along the road to Emmaus discussing their past and their future. Three years earlier they had chosen to follow the Teacher and now He was gone. They were between a rock and a hard place, stuck in between faith and doubt. Wanting to keep going but paralyzed with uncertainty. Then a stranger appeared and walked beside them. He enquired about their conversation and wondered why they were downcast. They did not recognize Him and assumed He was a foreigner because he seemed to know nothing of the events of the past week. He followed them to the city and had dinner with them. And when Jesus began to teach them, an amazing thing happened.

Their **eyes were opened,** and they recognized him. And they **arose up** that same hour. (vs. 31)

Two things happened in every story. First, their **eyes were opened**, and second, they **got up**!

Faith is the substance of things **hoped** for, the evidence of things **not seen**. And the only place to see the evidence is going through the rock and the hard place and scaling up to the peak. That is where our **eyes are opened**, and we see. We witness in panoramic view what was hidden to us below. We fight through the resistance of gravity and overcome our fear of inability. From below we hoped that if we reached the top then **perhaps** we would understand, and God would fight for us. And He does!

One of my favorite movies is The Cinderella Man. It is the rags-to-riches story of James Braddock, a one- time boxer now working as a day laborer during the Great Depression. He is approached by his former manager with an opportunity to go back into the ring against a rising young contender. After a shocking upset, he goes back to boxing full time and ultimately ends up in a championship fight. After originally struggling in his boxing career, he is interviewed before the title bout and asked the following question.

"What is different this time?" His response is as classic as his comeback.

"This time" said Braddock, "I know what I'm fighting for."

Rising Downward

A second chance and another chance are not the same thing. Another chance is when I give myself permission to try again. A second chance is when we are granted that privilege by someone else. Another chance can be immediate. A second chance takes time and the path forward may mean that I must first go back. This is called rising downward. **The path back is humility; there is no other path.**

Very often when people are seeking a second chance they want to begin where they are. But if you were climbing the wrong mountain you can't just jump to the right one. **The Climb** always begins at the bottom.

The golden rule on the Appalachian Trail is **Leave No Trace.** Whatever you pack in you must also pack out. Nothing annoys me more when I am hiking than litter. To see the natural landscape spoiled by empty bottles and cans makes my blood boil. If I could find the perpetrators, I would give them an orange vest and bag and make them pick up garbage for 100 miles. In life, people often leave a trail of debris scattered across not miles but across time. And because it is too humiliating to go back, bend down, and pick it up, they just want to move upward without rising downward. Their ego wants to push forward to the peak without having to go back down to the valley.

I don't like to retrace my steps when I hike. Usually my wife will drop me off and pick me up a few days later at a designated spot further up the trail. At times I will hike for 20 miles and then hitchhike back to my car. It seems like a waste of time to go back the same way when I could be moving forward and experiencing new things. There have been times, however, when that was necessary. In most of those cases it was for safety reasons. Maybe the weather was about to turn or darkness about to set in. On some hikes there was not an accessible pick up point or exit option. The way forward required going back. I didn't like it, but it had to be done.

When Jonathan began his climb, he knew what he was fighting for. When people are given a second chance to climb out from the rock and hard place, they must go back to remember what they had stopped fighting for. This is a crucial part of the process. You cannot return to the past or change the past, but the way forward is returning to the point where you got off onto the wrong path. Again, there are times when we find ourselves stuck through no fault of our own. But in the instances when we put ourselves in that position, we must not only reclimb, but also be ready to help others that we dragged down with us. And the depth of the hole is determined by the length of the fall. When Jonah found himself in the belly of the fish he exclaimed, "*The deep has surrounded me!*" He had not lost his faith, just his way. He chose not to follow his faith, and this did not please God. For him, the way back was going to be from the very lowest point he could imagine. And ultimately, he would find himself at the very crossroads where he had turned in the wrong direction.

What is your deep?

For Moses it was a desert, Joseph a prison, Elijah a cave, Daniel a den, Jonah a whale, Job a disability, Jesus a tomb. Some found themselves there through no fault of their own, others because of their own poor choices. And some, like Christ, placed themselves there voluntarily. The Bible says, "He humbled himself and became obedient to death."

Maybe your "deep" is a marriage, finances, health, or job. For some it might be a fear, a change, or a choice. The rock and hard place is a scary setting for many reasons. For one, the peak seems so high and insurmountable. The edges look sharp and jagged. We question our own ability to make the climb. Gravity is too much of a challenge. And what if we get halfway and fall again? Now, we can sit under the rock and consider and debate all day, but when we come to the end, we realize there are only two options; stay or climb. And we face the stark reality that there is only one direction: **UP!**

James described this as a person looking in the mirror and then walking away without acknowledging what they had seen. A dog looks in a mirror and sees another dog. A man looks in a mirror and sees the truth. But in the real world you do not get credit for just looking in the mirror.

There is also something else to consider. Jonathan realized this when he was in the same position. This climb was not just about him. There were other lives at stake. His band of brothers, family, and friends below needed inspiration. They thought a miracle was needed when all that was really required was a simple act of faith, for someone to do something that had their best interests at heart. An act of courage, an act of kindness, or an act of love. It is why Jonathan was the perfect choice for this mission.

Philippians 2—"*Do nothing out of selfish ambition but in humility, consider others better than yourselves.*" It is said of those listed in the Hall of Faith, "they did not seek their own."

Goats on the Roof

If you have ever driven through north Georgia or western Carolina or eastern Tennessee, you have probably seen this sign. It is a common attraction in the Appalachians and often associated with souvenir shops and ice cream stands. It is an attention grabber and tourists stop by the thousands to see goats literally walking on the roof. There is something instinctive in these creatures that drive them to climb. They need no motivation or encouragement. In fact, it would be cruel to not give them the opportunity.

This compulsion appears not to be instinctive in humans. Our desire to scale new heights often seems non-existent. We might do it with constant prodding but, even then, we do not like it. But the truth is we all are born with the yearning to climb. Unfortunately, we have become so domesticated we no longer recognize it. Why build it when we can buy it? Why earn it when it should be free? Our challenges are only virtual and aspirations only material. This, of course, is most often true in industrialized societies.

But it is also true of modern Christianity. We seem to be more interested in the Faith of our Fathers than in the future of our sons and daughters. We prefer a more sanitized version of faith. Climbing on our hands and feet will get dirt under our nails. Today's believers like to simply do their daily devotions and post something inspirational on social media. We much prefer our prayer closets and living rooms. Why would we want to climb on the roof?

Life often seems more like a circular pattern than a direction. We seem to be on a repetitive carousel—going to work, mowing the grass, getting a haircut, doing the laundry. Solomon's description of this is ***chasing the wind***. The thing about history is that it repeats itself, even in your own life, until you learn.

Mark Twain said, *"You don't learn anything the second time you are kicked by a mule."* But you do not learn anything new by simply repeating the old. Life is unpredictable. That may be why we find comfort in repetition; at least it is safe. Much like the new intersections now that have replaced stop signs with yield signs to create a congruent circle. If we stick to the routine, we will not get lost. Stick to the schedule and you never even have to look up, much less go up. Unfortunately, the mundane becomes the systemic problem that prevents us from going up. Cyclical patterns are familiar but keep us mired in the muck. Solomon wrote in Ecclesiastes that some people *"could live a thousand years and never be happy."*

One of our most famous Christmas carols is God Rest Ye Merry Gentlemen. The chorus contains the lyric, "good tidings of comfort and joy." Now there is nothing wrong with comfort. The Bible tells us to enjoy the fruit of our labor. But the fruit comes after the labor. The joy comes after the work. Paul told us in Philippians that Jesus, *"for the JOY that was set before him, endured the cross, despising the shame, and is now set down at the right hand of God."* The comfort and joy always have a toll. Venture out of the cul-de-sac. God always reveals the "right from wrong" morals, but not the "right from left" decisions. Clarity of direction comes from looking up.

Take a moment to consider the accounts of those who went up to meet with God. Moses went **Up** to Mt. Sinai to speak to God. Elijah went **Up** to Mt. Horeb to have a heart to heart conversation with God. Jesus took three disciples **Up** to a high mountain to witness the Transfiguration. The assumption might be that the mountaintop is closer to God. But that would be like saying if I get on my roof, I am closer to the sun. There is probably a better reason they all went Up. Could it be that these conversations were very private and needed a great deal of solitude? And if you need to go somewhere without a lot of people, go **UP**. There are very few on the peaks; most people do not care to climb. Instead they choose to play it safe, living under a false pretense of security. The illusion of a job, a house, or a routine become the same fragile rocks that the Israelites were hiding behind.

Overlook Just Ahead

There is nothing quite like a drive through the mountains in autumn. The magnitude of God's creation is breathtaking; His splendor is illuminated in the blaze of color. This sense of anticipation is heightened when we see a sign that alerts us to a clear overlook in the next mile. If you have ever driven on the Blue Ridge Parkway, there are numerous places when you are suspended above it all along a skyway bridge. My wife and grandson, Lucas, both have panic attacks in those moments. There are beautiful places you can only get to by crossing certain bridges. There are frightening truths we must face to arrive at magnificent locations of spirituality. Bridges are a great metaphor for faith and one of the great challenges in life is knowing what bridges to cross and what bridges to burn. But, do not let what you cannot understand destroy what you can enjoy.

Not long ago, our President declared a **National Emergency** due to the coronavirus. Almost immediately our stores emptied of toilet paper and hand sanitizer. Panic is a human trait that is so deeply seeded in our psyche that we usually forget it is there. But when unexpected fear invades, it erupts like a volcano.

Our response is often an overreaction, and, in the panic, we run in all directions as we strive for self-preservation. The **Covid-19 pandemic** taught us the difference between essential and non-essential jobs, but it also reminded us that there are no non-essential people. We were all between a rock and a hard place together. We were going to need to climb and by faith remember God's promise.

"God is able to bless you so that, in all things and at all times, you will have all you need." --2 Cor. 9:8

The Philistine response to Jonathan's unexpected strike was a classic **communal panic attack**. The garrison was caught off guard and they were completely unprepared for counter measures. Their lines of communication were completely broken down. What happened next no one could have anticipated. And no one was more surprised by what he saw than the armor-bearer.

"What is happening?" screamed the Philistine commander.

"We are not sure," replied his aide. "The reports are sketchy, but we are definitely under attack!"

"From where?"

"To the south," came the reply from a scout who had just entered the tent.

"How many are advancing?" the general demanded to know.

"We cannot tell, but they just engaged one of our garrisons."

"Casualties?"

The scout paused for a moment and then replied, "All of them, sir."

"All of them," said the commander. "How is that possible?" There was quiet in the tent.

Then the aide spoke up. "General, we have to get you out of here!"

"Yes. Yes, of course, but first we must alert our troops to withdraw."

The scout then confirmed the commander's worst fears. "They are already doing that, Sir."

"How could it have come to this?" the Philistine commander pondered. "We had the high ground, our army was superior, our strategy sound. How could we fall in just One Day?"

The scene from the valley was just as chaotic. The outpost guards of Israel were as confused as the Philistines as to what was happening. From a distance they could hear the screams and could see the enemy forces retreating but they had no idea why. Was another army attacking them from behind? Any number of theories began to formulate. And then their general arrived.

"Have we done a head count?" asked King Saul

"We are in the process now," he was told.

In a matter of minutes, the sergeant came in with the report.

"How many are out?" asked the king.

"Just two," was his response.

The general looked around and knew instantly that his men were thinking what he was thinking.

"Who?"

This time the response was slower in coming.

"Who?!"

Nervously the sergeant replied, "Your son, Jonathan, and his armor-bearer."

The king slowly shook his head.

"Why does that not surprise me?" he said curtly.

"What should we do?" someone bravely asked.

"Send this message to all our troops. On my order, we attack!"

Saul mustered his army and, when they arrived at the battle scene, they witnessed something that was both confusing and frightening. The Philistine soldiers were in such a panic they were engaging each other in combat. Not even sure who the enemy was anymore, they were doing what most people do in a panic: self-preservation. Saul's army entered the conflict knowing clearly who the enemy was and, for the first time in weeks, went on the offensive. Other companies from the hillsides soon joined in the skirmish and, in the shortest battle of the military campaign, the war was over. For Israel, that morning had begun amidst hopelessness and despair. By the end of the day the reporting war correspondent simply said, **"The Lord saved Israel that day."**

The annals of Jewish history are filled all too often with the horrors of war. Many ended in defiant victory, others in agonizing defeat. This war would not be the last with the Philistines. Many other valiant soldiers would arise in Israel to defend their country and their faith. But this battle, initiated by a man tired of being stuck between a rock and a hard place, would be remembered forever. Hundreds of years later Paul would remind us about what Jonathan did on that day:

He put to flight, the armies of aliens.

To every man there openeth a way and ways,

And some men climb the high way, and some men grope below

And in between on the misty flats the rest drift to and fro.

And to every man there openeth, a high way and a low;

And every man decideth, which way his soul shall go.

--John Oxenham

I Samuel 14

And the watchmen of Saul in Gibeah of Benjamin looked, and behold, the multitude was dispersing here and there. Then Saul said to the people who were with him, "Count and see who has gone from us." And when they had counted, behold, Jonathan and his armor-bearer were not there. Then Saul and all the people who were with him rallied and went into the battle. And behold, every Philistine's sword was against his fellow, and there was very great confusion. Now the Hebrews who had been with the Philistines before that time and who had gone up with them into the camp, even they also turned to be with the Israelites who were with Saul and Jonathan. Likewise, when all the men of Israel who had hidden themselves in the hill country of Ephraim heard that the Philistines were fleeing, they too followed hard after them in the battle. ***So, the Lord saved Israel that day.***

CHAPTER FOUR
OUT OF THE SHADOWS

"I went into the woods because I wanted to live deliberately and deep. To put to rest all that was not life and not, when I had come to the end of it, discover I had never really lived." Henry David Thoreau

When our grandson, Trey, was three years old, we took him to Burger King. I remember how excited he was about the indoor playground with all the tunnels to climb around in—until he got to the very top. The shriek he let out still chills us to this day. His grand-mommy and I did not know if he was frightened or hurt. He was crawling back down at light speed, screaming all the way. I met him at the bottom of the slide where he jumped into my arms exclaiming, "There's something in there!"

"What was it," I asked?

Trey replied, "I think it was an animal."

After consoling him with some ice cream, I decided to try and solve this mystery. And though it meant crawling through to the top of these small tunnels, we needed to know what it was that had terrified my grandson. As I neared the bend where he had seen the creature, I prepared myself for the worst. And as I made the turn and peered down the shaft, I realized what he had seen. It was his own shadow.

The light behind me shone through a plastic bubble and amplified a dark and sinister figure in the passageway below. When we told Trey that it was his shadow he asked, "What is a shadow?"

The day that Jonathan decided to come out of the shadows was the day a new light shined in Israel. It was not only a turning point in the war, it was also a defining moment in the relationship between him and his father. Saul's leadership was challenged for the first time that day and he would never be the same. The seed of jealousy and narcissism would now begin to characterize both him and his throne. This would eventually carry over to David, and the division would never be repaired. But that would come later. For now, Saul must deal with this tiny insurrection.

It is not a clinical diagnosis, but Saul exemplified many of the symptoms of bi-polar disorder. This used to be known as manic depressive. He demonstrated classic mood swings, difficulty thinking clearly, inflated ego, and impulsive behavior. Interestingly, it was David who would later relax the king by playing the harp. In retrospect, this may also be the reason that Samuel discouraged Israel from choosing him as their king. But it is also why Jonathan saw both the good and the bad in his father. And though he tried often to redeem him, eventually Saul would fall victim to the dark side.

Immediately following this unexpected victory, Saul once again gave in to impulsive behavior. He issued a decree that no one should eat anything until he gave further orders. Unfortunately, this news did not reach Jonathans ears. As the troops were moving through the forest looking for enemy stragglers, they came across a giant beehive, dripping with honey. Jonathan instinctively thrust in his spear and pulled up a piece of the honeycomb. After gulping down a heaping mouthful, his "eyes became bright." Now, I am not sure if that had spiritual significance, or if it was just a huge sugar rush. In any case, it was the catalyst for the first of many private and heated conversations between Jonathan and his father. In this instance, Saul took his son across the river to have a candid discussion.

"Why?" was the first question Saul had.

"Why what?" was Jonathans response, wanting his father to be specific.

"Why did you disobey my order and eat the honey?"

"To begin with," said his son, "I never heard that order. But if you want to get into this, the order didn't make sense."

"So," inquired Saul, "you would have disobeyed it anyway?"

"I guess we will never know," replied Jonathan. "But now, here we are."

"That's right! And you have put me between a rock and a hard place."

"Do whatever you think is right," Jonathan quipped.

"That seems very cavalier," Saul snapped back.

"That's because this is not the real question you want to ask, is it?"

"I don't know what you are talking about!"

"Yes, you do! This is not about honey."

"Then why don't you tell me what it is about," Saul questioned.

"You want to know why I secretly broke ranks and climbed that mountain without your permission."

"All right," said Saul, "let's have that conversation. Why did you disobey me?"

Jonathan took a moment. He knew his father well and that he was reaching a point of anger when he would make irrational decisions. Another course of action was needed to try and calm the direction that this debate was headed. Saul had asked the important question, "Why?" Jonathan decided to answer that question.

"When you were chosen as king, I was just a young boy. But I remember that day vividly, how proud I was of my father. The prophet Samuel didn't share my enthusiasm, but he heeded the people's request. And when he anointed you, it came with a charge to always follow. Do you remember what that challenge was?"

"No! Why don't you enlighten me!"

"This is what he said," and Jonathan recited it.

"Far be it from me that I should sin against the Lord by ceasing to pray for you, and I will instruct you in the good and the right way. Only fear the Lord and serve him faithfully with all your heart. For consider what great things he has done for you." (1 Samuel 12)

"I wasn't disobeying you," said Jonathan, "I was obeying God."

"That still...," but before Saul could finish, his son continued.

"Last night I couldn't sleep; I tossed and turned under this rock where I was hiding. This morning I woke up and Samuel's words came back to me. *'Serve God faithfully and consider what great things he has done for you.'* My choice to do what I did was not about you; it was between me and God. The climb was a test of my faith."

Saul hardly considered the sentiment.

"Nevertheless," he said, "you have left me without a choice. If I don't keep my word the people will think I chose nepotism over kingship. And so, you must die!"

The primary symptom that revealed itself in Saul's bipolar behavior was paranoia. The moment he took the throne, he was terrified that someone would take it from him. This is not to be confused with narcissistic behavior. That type of leader always feels threatened but not about their power. They are intimidated by the fear that someone might be better at something. They are not afraid of losing their title, only their influence and ultimately their control. In this instance, however, Saul wasn't concerned about stature, he was worried about statute.

Not long before, a very similar story had taken place, only that time, it had been Saul who had defeated the Philistines. Then he had many loyalists who wanted to put to death those who had been opposed to his leadership. But on the eve of his coronation, he issued a reprieve that no one would be put to death; this was a time of celebration. He was all too happy to declare this amnesty because it served him. But now he would not even consider a stay of execution for his own son. The previous precedent did not apply because it now had the potential to promote someone other than himself. This paranoia would define his leadership from this point forward. Many years later his successor's son, Solomon, wrote about the danger of this double standard in leadership. *"The integrity of the upright guides them but the unfaithful are destroyed by their duplicity."* (Proverbs 11)

What happened next the king could not have predicted. This usually happens when a leader loses perspective and believes that people should follow them by position rather than principle. One way to easily recognize this is when they believe that they are above the law and not accountable to their own standards. Ultimately, they will be challenged on this and their response will be extremely revealing. The narcissist will not tolerate it; the manic depressant will appear to accept it, but they will never forget it. It will be a seed whose roots grow deeper and deeper into fear and anxiety.

"Listen to me," shouted Saul. "I have a very painful announcement!"

The army gathered in formation before their general and their king.

"Though it brings me no pleasure, it has come to my attention that the law has been broken. My son, Jonathan, has confessed to this crime, and the penalty for this felony is death!"

There was a stunned silence in the ranks. Soldiers and civilians stared at each other in disbelief. It took several minutes to process the information. And then, almost in unison, came the reply.

"That's not going to happen!"

"I don't like it any better than you," Saul echoed back, "but that is the law."

"We don't accept that," he heard back. And then one individual bravely spoke for the crowd.

"Jonathan is the reason we are standing here. His bravery is what rescued us, and we will not allow one hair of his head to be harmed!"

"So, what do you propose?" asked the king.

"We demand a pardon!"

"Under what pretense?"

"Under mercy. Jonathan saved us, now we are going to save him."

Here was the first crisis of Saul's leadership. His authority was being challenged and his decision would have a profound effect on his government. He had been chosen because of his charisma, which is simply a fancy word for ego. Pride is the worst trait in a leader. Moses was arguably the greatest human leader ever and simultaneously was the meekest man on the earth. One would think that Saul would be ecstatic about the life of his son being spared. Sadly, that probably had no bearing on the words he spoke next.

"So be it," was the only pragmatic thing he could say.

So, the people ransomed Jonathan

Heroism is more of a lifestyle than a single act. It may often reveal itself in a momentary act of bravery, but it is always there just below the surface. Jonathan's decision to emerge out of the shadows that day was the culmination of a life dedicated to doing what is right. Courage is a conscious choice to defend your conviction and to speak your voice. That can be done with words, but it is far more effective with action. **Faith is putting action to our voice.** It is easier to remain in the shadow, but that sentiment is completely foreign to what Jesus taught. *"No one hides a candle under a bushel; so, let your light shine before men that they might see your good works and glorify your Father."*

The heroic life is one of continual acts of love and faith. We often designate it to soldiers and first responders but, realistically, it is a response to every endeavor of our life. In marriage, family, vocation,

decision, and direction, faith is a demonstration of Whom we believe more than what we believe. **Because without**

faith it is impossible to prove what we believe. This is the enormous disconnect between faith and belief. Believing in God and in what He can do is a far distant cry from what we, by faith, allow Him to do. **It is the expanse from the bottom of the mountain to the pinnacle, from shadow to light.**

Does your shadow follow you or lead you?

Consider this. The only way we can see our shadow is to turn away from the light. If you are following your shadow it is leading you away from the light. And when you are far enough from the light the shadow simply disappears. Without any markers, we lose our sense of direction and that place becomes our existence, surrounded by shady characters. We reside on the planet but not in it. Why would you want to live in the shadowlands, in the gray existence of half-truths and half-lives? Jesus dreams of so much more for us than this. We are supposed to be the radiance of His life and it does not reflect well in the shadows.

Some have convinced themselves that if they are facing the light they are in the light. Or that because they are not totally in the dark, the shadows are not that bad. They may be facing the light but are slowly walking backwards. Those who live in the shadows must manage the gravitational pull between light and dark. The shadow is not a static existence. That is why Jesus taught, "Walk in the light while you have the light so that you are not overcome by the darkness."

We used to sing an old hymn in the small church where I grew up. The chorus was very simple and the message very clear. People would sing it with heartfelt emotion, not even realizing it was a vow.

"Where He leads me, I will follow, where He leads me, I will follow, where He leads me, I will follow,

No turning back, no turning back." The problem with the sentiment was that no one was really going anywhere. Scripture gives a clear mandate when it comes to following. We are to "live by faith" and "walk by faith." Nothing about either of those allows you to compartmentalize your faith. It permeates all you do and the decisions you make.

When Peter met with Christ for their final conversation, his Teacher left him with these haunting words. *"When you were young you went where you wanted, but when you are old another will lead you where you would not go."* We are then afforded the luxury, which Peter was not, of the significance of this statement. Jesus was, of course, referring to Simon Peter's appointment with death. This would not be a sentence meted out by God. It would come from a world that is opposed to God. A world that is acrimonious to the subject of faith. A world that chooses self over others and darkness over light.

When you cut corners, take shortcuts, and spin the truth, you walk in the shadows. That is not something you want everyone to know about or reveal on social media. The shadow world is one where we constantly strive for concealment.

Appointments are, by their very nature, terrifying. Maybe it is with the doctor, or dentist, or tax accountant, or mechanic. It could be for a job interview, a blind date, or a court hearing. In any case, the angst that arises is almost debilitative. It is marked clearly on the calendar, which only intensifies the dread as the date approaches. And this terror is what causes most cancellations and why so many businesses must charge a cancellation fee. I call this fee a **fear tax**.

We all know that we each have an appointment with death, but none have the date on the calendar. Those with a terminal illness are given a time frame, but not a day or hour. All of us suffer from the terminal illness of sin. In the 90th Psalm we are told that our diagnosis is on average 70-80 years. The reason that the Great Physician doesn't tell us our expiration date is because He does not want us to live in fear, He wants us to live in faith. He wants us to lead full, rich, happy, and meaningful lives filled with love and joy. His desire is to bless us beyond measure and give us opportunities to make a difference in the world. His hope is that we will climb and move mountains.

There is another appointment that we each must face, and it is one that is critical to my Core Beliefs-- we will all give our **own** account to God. We will give our own account because we were given our own race to run and mountain to climb. Solomon, at the end of his search for meaning in life, came to one stark conclusion to the matter: *"Fear God and keep his commandments, for this is the whole duty of mankind. For God will bring every deed into judgement, including every secret thing, whether it is good or evil."* That appointment cannot be cancelled or postponed and there are only two possible verdicts.

"You of little faith," or "Well done, good and faithful servant."

Jonathan's enemy was not really the Philistines, it was what they stood for: oppression, injustice, and intolerance. This was not simply a battle for land it was a war of ideology, a conflict of good and evil. It was a contest between his God and theirs, and the winner would determine whose truth was more powerful. Sometimes victory comes in overwhelming fashion, sometimes disguised by agonizing defeat. Faith is fighting for truth and justice, by life or by death. This is not to say that Jonathan had no sense of dread about this maneuver. It may have followed him all the way up the mountain, and for many it catches up to them along the way. **Fear kills more dreams than failure ever will.**

Jonathan had to make that climb because he had to know. He was perfectly willing to die at the hands of the Philistines if that would bring victory to his family. He was perfectly willing to be martyred by his own father if that would advance the truth among his people. To live by faith and walk by faith might ultimately mean to die by faith. Most of us have never been put in that situation and hope we never will. Fortunately, that is not God's will for most of us. But He does have a blueprint for each of us. The final design will look different, but the building strategy will be the same: live and walk by faith.

The faith to move mountains often comes with the courage to climb them.

Saul's Rash Vow

*I Samuel 14--And the men of Israel had been hard pressed that day, so Saul had laid an oath on the people, saying, "Cursed be the man who eats food until it is evening and I am avenged on my enemies." So, none of the people had tasted food. Now when all the people came to the forest, behold, there was honey on the ground. And when the people entered the forest, behold, the honey was dropping, but no one put his hand to his mouth, for the people feared the oath. But Jonathan had not heard his father charge the people with the oath, so he put out the tip of the staff that was in his hand and dipped it in the honeycomb and put his hand to his mouth, and **his eyes became bright**. Then one of the people said, "Your father strictly charged the people with an oath, saying, 'Cursed be the man who eats food this day.'" And the people were faint. Then Jonathan said, "My father has troubled the land. See how my eyes have become bright because I tasted a little of this honey. How much better if the* *people had eaten freely today of the spoil of their enemies that they found. Now the defeat among the Philistines has not been great."*

And Saul inquired of God, "Shall I go down after the Philistines? Will you give them into the hand of Israel?" But he did not answer him that day. And Saul said, "Come here, all you leaders of the people, and know and see how this sin has arisen today. For as the Lord lives who saves Israel, though it be in Jonathan my son, he shall surely die." But there was not a man among all the people who answered him. Then he said to all Israel, "You shall be on one side, and I and Jonathan my son will be on the other side." And the people said to Saul, "Do what seems good to you." Therefore Saul said, "O Lord God of Israel, why have you not answered your servant this day? If this guilt is in me or in Jonathan my son, O Lord, God of Israel, give Urim. But if this guilt is in your people Israel, give Thummim." And, Jonathan and Saul were taken, but the people escaped. Then Saul said, "Cast the lot between me and my son Jonathan." And Jonathan was taken. Then Saul said to Jonathan, "Tell me what you have done." And Jonathan told him, "I tasted a little honey with the tip of the staff that was in my hand. Here I am; I will die." And Saul said, "God do so to me and more also; you shall surely die, Jonathan." Then the people said to Saul, "Shall Jonathan die, who has worked this great salvation in Israel? Far from it! As the Lord lives, there shall not one hair of his head fall to the *ground, for he has worked with God this day." So, **the people ransomed Jonathan**, so that he did not die.*

CHAPTER FIVE
THIRD TIER LEADERSHIP

"If you can't be a tree, be a bush. If you can't be a highway, just be a trail. If you can't be a sun, be a star. It isn't by size that you win or fail. Just be the best of whatever you are." –Martin Luther King

The greatest acts of faith are those that have no precedent. No one has gone before or maybe no one has succeeded before. Moses knew this when he stood before the Red Sea. David felt it when he stood before the giant. Peter understood it when he got out of the boat. Each of these men were given the mantle of leadership, not because of their exploits, but because of their **risk of faith**. They didn't necessarily want it, but they assumed it. Some say that people are born to leadership, that you can see it in them at an early age. But maybe that is not leadership; maybe what we are witnessing is arrogance.

It might not be leadership at all, just the all-consuming need for attention.

If you were to do a comparative research study on leaders and followers, you would find great disparity. There are thousands of books and quotes on leadership, very few about followers. In fact, followers are often disdained by leaders, as if there is something wrong with them if they do not pursue leadership. In modern circles you are almost deemed a failure if you do not strive to be a leader. And yet, when Jesus chose the twelve, He said, "Follow me." He did not say to them, "I will make you leaders of men." He said, "I will make you fishers of men." To be sure, leadership is essential. Where we make our mistake is to confuse **The Climb** with the rise to leadership, as if that is the goal.

Jonathan was not trying to make a name for himself; he never did. His climb was not some strategical move up the power ladder. Remember, he didn't disclose to anyone what he was doing. The only person he was concerned about leading was himself. This does not always sit well with the leadership movement. Leaders feel like failures if they don't have next generation executives and associates.

Saul assumed that Jonathan was the presumptive future king, the rightful heir to the throne. What he could never understand was that Jonathan **did not want it!** The problem was that Saul saw leadership from the throne position. Everything rises and falls on leadership, but tragically there is as much falling as there is rising. King Saul was about to learn this lesson. Over the next few years, he would attempt to strengthen his grip on power only to see it continually decline until eventually his legacy was sealed with the following words: *"See how the mighty have fallen."*

Followers are more important to leaders than leaders are to followers.

You never hear that at a leadership conference, do you? We learn all about leadership styles, and vision casting, and personal development. It is overwhelmingly focused on the leader, not the follower. We tell ourselves that we want to be better leaders because that will be good for the followers. And maybe that is true in the beginning, but most lose sight of that along the way. The most important leadership principle Jesus taught was that He had come to serve, not be served. In fact, He was never referred to as the leader of the disciples. He was their Master, a term referring to him as mentor and teacher. We assume He was their leader because they were His followers. But it is not always a simple binary system.

For Paul, the most important quality of leadership was **authenticity**, not title. Each and every time he commended someone in leadership it was for how they had helped and encouraged others. Not how many they had baptized or how big was their church, but how they had humbly given their lives to make a difference in the lives of others. He demanded that people would not look at them or their authority, but to observe the tangible outcomes of their faith and lives and to imitate that. Were their relationships healthy? Was their reputation honorable? Did they exemplify power or humility? Were they more concerned with talking or listening? Were they patient or easily angered? Did they have the interests of others at heart or were they more concerned about their own legacy. And Paul found himself often in his writings warning people not to show favor and partiality to the charismatic or wealthy. People often confuse popularity with leadership, but the Apostle wrote, *"Remember your leaders who have spoken God's word to you. As you carefully observe the **outcome** of their lives, **imitate** their faith."* Hebrews 13:7

Self-leadership

The most important principle of self-leadership is "Knowing who you are and are not." It is one of the most recognizable traits of Johnathan. He knew better than anyone that he was not created to be king.

He had an undying loyalty to those in that position, but knew clearly that he was not that person. He knew who he was, and he was completely comfortable in his own skin. He did not toot his own horn or serve as president of his own fan club. Leaders would do well to identify those in their organizations who fit that description and remember that they are most likely the greatest influencers.

Several years ago, Dos Equis created a figurehead known as The Most Interesting Man in the World. He was a debonair gentleman who was the life of the party, even at parties he didn't attend. He won the lifetime achievement award...twice. He could speak Russian...in French. His mother had a tattoo that said, "Son." And there was one piece of advice he gave that I have never forgotten. "In life, you must find the things you do not do well, and then don't do those things." That is memorable.

Over time I have observed scores of people strive to become leaders who had no business in that position. They attempt to accomplish things they just are not capable of doing. There were a myriad of others coerced and pressured into leading who never wanted it in the first place. But in the **leadership construct** they were taught that this was the natural order. In the business world it is referred to as the corporate ladder and it comes with titles, perks, and increased income. Now, that is not necessarily a bad thing, until it gets to the point of seeing others further down the rungs as less than vital.

The Biblical role of leadership looks quite different. During the time of Samuel, the prophet, the people decided that they wanted a king, a leader of their own choosing. This idea is not bad in principle, it's just that he knew the ulterior motives of the people. And when they chose Saul, the most charismatic man who stood head and shoulders above the crowd, Samuel realized that this was not a good idea. However, he was directed by God to allow this change in polity as a standard for future generations. For the next several hundred years Israel would be ruled by both good and evil monarchs. Each of them had tiers and layers of leaders and followers below them. Many were people with their own power-hungry schemes of advancement. Others were loyalists, completely at ease with who and where they were in the process. The sheep and the wolves as it were. In the corporate world it is usually the wolves who advance, but in God's kingdom it works very differently.

Third Tier Leaders

Moses, Joshua, **Caleb**

Saul, David, **Jonathan**

Peter, James, **John**

Paul, Barnabas, **Epaphroditus**

Adino, chief of the three; Eleazar, next to him; and **Shammah** (David's mighty men)

Mary, Mary Magdalene, and **The Other Mary**

Caleb knew his role and was comfortable in it. He accepted Joshua's title and supported him fully. In return, all he asked for was a single mountain. John was not as fiery as Peter or James but watched them both die and was then tasked with recording the Revelation. David's mighty men were soldiers with designated military positions. They were divided into two groups, our version of Rangers and Seals. Each division had their top three commanders who had attained their positions by their exploits. Their rank was specifically mentioned by the historian who recorded the events. In the first group was Adino, chief of the three. Next to him was Eleazer. After him was Shammah who, single-handedly defeated a troop of Philistines. The other group had a soldier named Benaiah (who faced the lion), listed in the third position of his peers. It is said that he did not attain to the first three, but his contribution was crucial to the cause.

We know full well the role that Paul was called to and why. We also are aware that Barnabas' name was almost synonymous with his, at least in the early years of the church. But there was a third member of Paul's team who Paul went out of his way to make sure people remembered. The reason was because Epaphroditus knew who he was and fulfilled his role in the way that was most natural for him. And then there were the three Mary's: the mother of Christ, the Magdalene, and the Other Mary. How would you like to be known throughout history as the Other one? She was and was completely comfortable with it.

First tier leaders tend to be linear thinkers. They see leadership in a very binary fashion. *"My way or the highway,"* they like to say, and *"Think outside the box."* The organizations and churches they oversee are measured statistically by individual numbers, members, baptisms, and money. Pastors write sermons with three points. First tier leaders see life as a framework of lines and rules. They can grasp secondary roles like protégé, vice-president and executive associate. But it is difficult for them to comprehend third tier leaders; their minds just do not work like that.

Third tier leaders tend to be creative. They think outside the circle. These individuals have an ability to conceptualize, to devise strategies and goals that do not necessarily follow structural norms. First tier leaders are the visionaries; third tier leaders are the dreamers, the ones who make the vision happen.

Caleb could see a mountain and remember it 40 years later. It was John who was chosen to write the Revelation because his creative mind could put words to the unimaginable images he would see. It was the Other Mary who would anoint the feet of Jesus while others said, "What a waste." It was a third level member of David's mighty men who went into a pit to kill a lion. And it was Jonathan who realized that standard military tactics were not accomplishing the mission and saw a different alternative.

Jonathan understood that the throne was not his and he did not aspire to it. In leadership circles that might be looked on as shirking his responsibility. Others might say he didn't become all that he could be. And narcissistic leaders scratch their head because it just does not compute with them.

The part of their behavior that puzzles top tier leaders most is a third tier's loyalty to conviction. This is in complete contrast to many leaders I have known whose leadership style is that of **expedience**: compromising conviction and character for necessity or gratification or attention. It is, again, searching for the easier path, the blue blazed trail. They only reward loyalty that follows their agenda and are, in fact, not very loyal themselves. This story played out in the lives of Saul and Jonathan in the years after **The Climb**.

The greatest rock and hard place for Jonathan was the position between his father and his king. He was loyal to his commander, though with open eyes. But as a son, he was guilty of doing what many sons do. He was often blinded by love for his dad and a desire to earn his respect. As a soldier he would courageously defy orders to do what was right. As a son, he took a different approach to the paternal order of things. These appear to be inconsistencies, but for Jonathan they were completely coherent. He never attempted to correct the king; he tried often to redeem his father. Most of the mitigation that Jonathan was involved in was between Saul and David. The king saw David as threat, Jonathan embraced him as his best friend. Saul, as most narcissists do, saw this as disloyalty and it infuriated him.

"Where is David?" asked Saul. "Why is he not eating with us?"

Jonathan answered, "He asked my permission to go celebrate the holiday with his family."

Saul tried to contain himself but could not. "Your permission?" he asked sarcastically.

"Yes," was his son's reply. "He wanted to go to Bethlehem, and I sent him with my blessing,"

It is often hard to know when someone with bi-polar disorder is symptomatic or just angry. In this situation I believe it was the latter. In any case, Saul was irate!

"You son of a perverse, rebellious woman! I know that you have chosen the son of Jesse to your own shame, and to the shame of your mother."

So, wait a minute! Saul has just called Jonathan's mother an evil witch, but then accuses Jonathan of shaming her? That is how the irrational mind works. His next words reveal how narcissism works.

"Don't you know that every day David lives on the earth is a threat to the throne and your kingship?!"

There it is. The Spin. The Deflection. Narcissistic leaders hone that skill to perfection. Saul could not throw a spear straight, but he could bend and manipulate the truth to his own satisfaction. This was about power and control. And lessen #1 to Jonathan was going to be how to keep it at any cost. Sacrifice family, friends, morals, and character if need be, but do not lose control!

"Bring David to me now," shouted the king! "He must die!!!"

Jonathan answered, "WHY? What has he done?"

There it is. The pushback. The need to know and understand. Show me the logic. Second and third tier leaders are ready to perform their duty but just want to make sense of it first. If they see the clarity, they will run through walls to make it happen. But the vision must be clear to them.

> *"If you want to inspire people you must give them a vision that is positive for them."* --Martin Luther King

The Why question is what separates an authentic leader from an artificial one. And the response of the leader will tell the tale. Saul's response was to take his spear and hurl it at Jonathan. We know how proficient David was with a sling and Jonathan with a bow. This was the third time Saul threw his spear, twice at David, and now at his own son, and he missed every time. You would think he would choose a different weapon. Granted, he was probably drunk, but what really caused his aim to be off was his anger.

Everyone has a hot button. For narcissistic leaders it is the Why question. Their paranoia leads them to believe that someone is challenging their authority when what they are doing is questioning their judgement. Authentic leaders will surround themselves with second and third tier leaders who possess wisdom and discernment about decisions that affect many people. Instead, far too many surround themselves with other narcissists or with leaders who will not question anything. This way they can simply lead by executive order. This was Saul, he was the King, and that was that.

The reaction that a leader shows when asked for an explanation is quite revealing. If anger is the typical response, there is something wrong with their character. They may show it in different ways, but you can see it in their countenance. And though they may not physically throw things, there will be a lot of hurling none-the-less. It may be words, insults, threats, or repercussions, but things will be flying.

Saul's response was predictable, Jonathan's was quite atypical. It would be humorous if not so tragic. Some of us just don't catch on right away. It takes several incidents before we can accept the truth. Often, we simply don't see it; at other times we are in denial about it. This is most often true of parents toward their children. In Jonathan's case it was the opposite. He continued clinging to the hope that circumstances would improve, that his father would have a change of heart. He had watched Saul's attacks on others, but now, for the first time, the attack was directed at him. That was the turning point; it was **then** he knew for certain.

It is a painful moment to lose faith with someone you want to believe in. Jonathan had been fighting this war between his father and David for a long time. It had taken a great emotional toll on him. There were moments when he thought they had turned a corner, only to slip and fall. This climb had been far more complicated than he had ever imagined. Now it had finally reached its climax, and this time Jonathan realized he had lost the battle. That does not mean he should not have attempted the climb. To do that is to give up hope, and faith is the substance of the things we hope for. Jonathan fought for his father because, **"perhaps"** he would change. But that is not a guarantee.

The Plot 'Not' to Overthrow

The sad irony to Saul's paranoia was that David and Jonathan were scheming the exact opposite outcome. It was the conspiracy theory that never existed. Their hope was that Saul would finally repeal David's death sentence and grant him a stay of execution. The strategy was for Jonathan to confront his father one last time and demand clemency. The next day he would meet David in an empty field and use a series of signal arrows to make David aware of the King's intentions. Jonathan was extremely proficient with his craft. He was the first Avenger, the Hawkeye of his time. He would bring a young boy with him to gather the arrows, but the boy was never in any danger and completely oblivious to the real scenario that was taking place. He sent his arrows beyond the boy which alerted David that his sentence was not commuted. After that Jonathan sent the boy away.

This is another fascinating insight into Jonathan's character. He did not want to endanger the boy. Should this plot of betrayal ever become known to Saul, this lad would not be culpable in it. As far as he knew, he was simply gathering arrows from his master's target practice. Jonathan was never afraid of the consequences of his own actions but sought to protect others from his choices. That young boy would grow into manhood never actually knowing what happened in the field that day. These are the types of examples that make me admire Jonathan. The heir to the throne who chose instead to follow his own heart and his own path. That is how he lived, and that is how he died.

Once the boy was out of sight, he met David in the field. The embrace of the two friends was not disturbed with words; they knew this may be the last time they would see each other. They both wept, but David's tears flowed most. And then the silence was broken.

"You have to go now," said Jonathan. "My father will soon realize my absence."

"I'm sorry I came between the two of you," lamented David.

"It was never about you. He has been ill for a long time. You remember that from the times you would play your music to calm him. But his paranoia grew like a cancer."

They each turned to walk away. David took two steps, then paused and said, "Hey?"

Jonathan tilted his head to the side. "What?"

David slowly turned around. "I never asked you. Why did you not want the throne?"

His friend did not turn but lifted his head to the sky. "It's not a mystery really, it's just not who I am. But I could never make my father understand that."

"I think Saul wanted it desperately for you," David surmised.

"No," responded Jonathan. And then looking back down said, "He wanted it for himself, for his legacy.

I think he always believed that he had failed somehow."

David thought carefully about that sentiment for a moment and then tried to encourage his best friend.

"Just so you know, I think you would have been an exemplary king and well-loved among our people."

Now Jonathan turned and looked eye to eye. "They will love you more. And they will follow you because they admire you. Not because you killed a giant but because you were the only one willing to try."

"That was a long time ago. And by the way, I know you could have killed Goliath with your bow. What was that about?"

Jonathan laughed. "I remember the first time my father took me deer hunting. On the first day we came upon a huge stag, larger than any my dad had ever killed. I told him that he should take the shot because I might miss. He said, "No, son. That's your deer!"

"That's a great story," remarked David. "Is there a point to it?"

"Goliath was your giant," Jonathan replied. "We all have them, and no one can fight them but us." "Besides," he continued, "my father was offering his daughter, and the victor would never pay taxes again. I couldn't marry my sister and I was the king's son; I've never paid taxes. So, there wasn't anything in it for me."

At first David smiled, but then it turned to a grin as he pondered if that was really, true. At any rate he was happy for the levity in the conversation.

"I worry sometimes that I will follow in Saul's footsteps."

"You won't," said Jonathan.

"How can you be sure?" David wanted to know.

"Because no one knows you better than I do. My father was elected by the people. You were chosen by God. Samuel warned them what a king could become. You will show them **what a king should be**.

And besides, there is one thing you have that always escaped my father."

"What is that" David enquired.

"FAITH!" Jonathan replied with a wry grin.

"What will you do now?" asked David.

"Well, for one, I've met a girl. We plan to get married and start a family. I would love to have a boy one day. Until then I will do what I have always done: serve my king and fight for my people."

"Shalom, my friend. I look forward to meeting your son one day."

Go in Peace, my brother," echoed Jonathan. "And remember our pledge. Our bond is not just between us. It will carry down to our descendants." Jonathan reached out his hand and they clasped arms.

"You have my word," replied the future king. "In life or in death."

Then Jonathan turned and went back into the city.

Later that evening...

A woman calls her son in for supper. As they sit to eat the boy's mother asks,

"What did you do today?"

"Not much," the boy replied. "Just went target shooting with the king's son."

"Did he hit anything?" asked his father.

"No. Just shot some arrows into an empty field."

"Sounds very uneventful," replied his mother.

"I guess," replied the boy.

"Alright," said his father. "Finish your supper now, Uriah."

Over the next few years David and Jonathan would only see each other one more time. Saul would engage in a never-ending quest to take David's life. He, in turn, would spare the king's life on three different occasions. David's fame and followers grew stronger and stronger. Meanwhile, Jonathan married the young girl and eventually they did have a son whom they named Mephibosheth. Israel would continue their conflict with the Philistines for decades to come. But fate would eventually catch up with Saul and his sons. Their mortal enemies would finally defeat them in battle. They would grotesquely display the king's body in public and strip Jonathan of his armor. But they would never be able to extinguish the memory of the day that "Jonathan put the armies of the aliens to flight."

1 Samuel 31:2--And the Philistines overtook Saul and his sons, and the Philistines struck down Jonathan and Abinadab and Malchi-shua, the sons of Saul.

In the end, Jonathan died beside his father in battle. David would include this important item in the song he would later write about their deaths, *"See how the mighty have fallen."* It would serve as a tribute to Jonathan's loyalty both to his father, Saul, and his friend, David. These men would be the two **metaphorical cliffs** on either side of his life. To fight simultaneously for what you love and for what is right. There are times when faith will force us to pick a side. To choose between what is known and comfortable for what is true and noble. To search our hearts and to know the will of God. To seek out wisdom for the assurance that we are climbing the right mountain.

It was Joshua, on the precipice of his climb, that reminded the people who were about to embark on the next phase of their own history, this important truth.

"IF you seek Him you will find Him…IF you seek Him with all your heart and with all your soul."

1 Samuel 20—

Then Saul's anger was kindled against Jonathan, and he said to him, "You son of a perverse, rebellious woman, do I not know that you have chosen the son of Jesse to your own shame, and to the shame of your mother." But Saul hurled his spear at him to strike him. Then Jonathan knew that his father was determined to put David to death. And Jonathan rose from the table in fierce anger and ate no food the second day of the month, for he was grieved for David, because his father had disgraced him.

In the morning Jonathan went out into the field to the appointment with David, and with him a little boy. And when the boy came to the place of the arrow that Jonathan had shot, Jonathan called after the boy and said, "Is not the arrow beyond you?" And Jonathan called after the boy, "Hurry! Be quick! Do not stay!" So, Jonathan's boy gathered up the arrows and came to his master. But the boy knew nothing. Only Jonathan and David knew the matter.

CHAPTER SIX
A ROCK AND A HARD PLACE

"The purpose of life is to be defeated by greater and greater things. Let everything happen to you: beauty and terror. Just keep going. No feeling is final." –Rainer Maria Rilke

A life in three verses

There is a story found in the book of 2 Chronicles that I have always found humorous. It is the short synopsis about the life of a man named **Abijah**. The comedy is found in the short order of events that describe his epitaph. I can just imagine someone reading this bio at his funeral. It is found in chapter thirteen; that alone should be an omen. In the first verse it is recorded that Abijah grew strong and mighty. In the third verse we read that Abijah slept with his fathers, and they buried him in the city of David. Now, how do you go from being strong and mighty to dead in just two verses? The answer is found in the verse in between. And he took fourteen wives and had twenty-two sons and sixteen daughters. Yep, that will do it! There is a lot of stress between the rock and the hard place.

Faith will **intentionally** place us between a rock and a hard place. Jesus often acknowledged that with the words, "This is a hard saying…." Not an impossible choice, just a difficult one. A classic example of this is the following story. A rich man came to Jesus and asked the supreme question, "What must I do to inherit eternal life?"

"Keep the commandments" Jesus replied. (That is the **Rock**)

"I have kept them from my youth," responded the man.

"Then there is only one thing you lack," said Christ. "Go and sell all you have and give it to the poor." (That is the **Hard Place**.)

The man went away sorrowful, for he had much wealth. The point Jesus was making was that his money would always keep him from the one thing he needed most to please God—Faith.

There are many phrases that often get confused with "a rock and a hard place." It is important not to muddle their meanings. If they are used in the wrong context, they will not offer hope, only despair. Particularly when they are misconstrued with the subject of faith. There will be times when we find ourselves in difficult situations, but there is always a way out and a way up; always a **way of escape**. Our enemy does not want us to believe that and so he offers different alternatives to our dilemma.

Catch 22—The main tenet of this expression is that there is no way out, no possible outcome that brings positive results. The worst is inevitable. Often this leads us to a victim mentality. We have all witnessed this disease among family and friends. It is catastrophic to live with no hope.

Six of One, Half Dozen of the Other-- The central idea of this expression is that either choice will bring the same result. Stay or go, up or down, left or right will make no difference. The greatest danger we make in this scenario is to do nothing. We bide our time and let circumstances ultimately dictate our direction. We abdicate our free will to the snare of apathy.

The Lesser of Two Evils—I can climb to the top or stay at the bottom. It seems like neither are good options, so we choose the lesser, what we deem to be the safer or the easier. The rich man chose what he assumed was the safer route. The trap of this ideology is that we assume the climb is the enemy when in fact the incline is our salvation. It is the struggle that makes us strong, that builds our muscle and cardio and stamina.

Taking the High Ground

This may be the most overlooked part of Jonathan's story. When we get to the top of the mountain we want to rest and enjoy the view. For Jonathan and his aide, that is when the fight began. It would have been much easier if the enemy had come down. We much prefer to fight them on our terms and in terrain with which we are familiar. Our strategy is to shoot from behind a rock and out of view. We throw darts and then retreat. We throw rocks from glass houses. But what we never, ever do is confront the enemy face to face. Especially when we are outnumbered. That would require faith.

Let's talk practically about this life of faith, remembering that it is impossible to please God without it. What are some of the most challenging climbs we will face? What are some of the most terrifying obstacles and heights that take our breath away? Which are the ones that cause us to question God the most? What are the mountains that make us believe we are better off down below? **We cannot ascend to the foothills and think we have climbed the mountains.** To love our neighbor is one thing, to love our enemy another. To forgive once is challenging, to forgive a thousand seems impossible. To judge others is an easy climb, to judge ourselves is a view we don't want to see. To live by my timing is to climb on my terms; to live by God's timing is to follow his will. To live for myself is exhilarating; to die to self is terrifying. But that is the way **UP!**

A Rock and a Hard Place: Love Your Enemies

It was Jesus who first initiated this proclamation and command. And what better person to do so, having never been an enemy himself. He was crystal clear that He had not come to condemn or destroy, but to heal and save anyone who would believe. His time for defeating foes would be in our far distant future; for now, He offers an alternative world view. The Apostle Paul also gave clear and exact detail as to the specifics of loving our enemy. This is from the opposite continuum, having been the former enemy of Christ. Interestingly the Apostle Peter doesn't speak to the issue. Maybe because he had found himself in the middle of the two sides; maybe it was a climb too high for him to make. After first resisting, maybe taking the gospel to the Gentiles was the highest form of love he could muster. But do not be harsh with him. Most of us are more like Peter than we care to admit.

So, what are the particulars of this rock and hard place? Jesus told his disciples to love their neighbor and their enemy and their response was, "Who is my neighbor?" They didn't ask about the enemies; their identity was extremely clear. When Jonathan was making his climb, he knew his mortal enemies would be waiting on top. There was no guessing as to the strategy: kill or be killed. The eye for an eye mentality comes naturally to us. It is our favorite part of the Old Testament. It makes much more rational sense in our psyche. The enemy should get what they deserve.

We love the stories of God's revenge when the bullies get what is coming to them. Who could not cheer when Elijah reigned down fire on evil prophets? We applauded when Pharaoh's army was drowned in the sea, and gave a standing ovation when Jezebel was thrown off the tower and eaten by dogs. We rooted for Samson when he pushed down the walls, and roared for David when the stone hit Goliath between the eyes. We laughed when the Philistines were smitten with hemorrhoids, felt little remorse when Judas hung himself, and felt vindicated when Herod was eaten alive by worms. The more graphic the ending, the sweeter the revenge. We want instant justice with extreme prejudice to those who do wrong. We want the Rambo, Braveheart, and Gladiator finale!

Remember the story we alluded to earlier with Elisha and his servant? When his eyes were opened, he saw God's army had surrounded the Syrians. Many of you think the slaughter that came next was horrific and well deserved. It might surprise you to know what really transpired.

2 Kings 6—Just deserts?

And when the Syrians came down against him, Elisha prayed to the Lord and said, "Please strike this people with blindness." So, he struck them with blindness in accordance with the prayer of Elisha. And Elisha said to them, "This is not the way, and *this is not the city. Follow me, and I will bring you to the man whom you seek." And he led them to Samaria. As soon as they entered Samaria, Elisha said, "O Lord, open the eyes of these men, that they may see." So, the Lord opened their eyes and they saw, and behold, they were in Samaria. As soon as the king of Israel saw them, he said to Elisha, "My father, shall I strike them down? He answered, "You shall not strike them down. Would you strike down those whom you have taken captive with your sword and with your bow? Set bread and water before them, that they may eat and drink and go to their master." So he prepared for them a great feast, and when they had eaten and drunk, **he sent them away**, and they went to their master. And the Syrians did not come again on raids into the land of Israel.*

Some of you are now disappointed. What a waste of an opportunity you may think. We had them surrounded and we let them go. Yet, in a nutshell, that is what loving our enemy is: **letting them go**.

But not just releasing them; that would be hard enough. Elisha prepared a great feast for them. You might need to read again the 23rd Psalm. When we are in the presence of our enemy, it was God who prepared the table. Jesus said that if you only love those who love you, what reward do you expect?

The guidelines to loving our enemies are made very clear. This climb may seem torturous, filled with thorns. The rocks may seem jagged and sharp but, remember, it is your own freedom and future you are seeking. Here is the ravine that we must scale.

--Pray for them

--Forgive them

--Bless them

--Do not curse them

--Do good to them

--Lend to them without expecting anything in return

--Turn the other cheek

--If he is hungry feed him; if he is thirsty give him something to drink

--Do not repay evil for evil

--Do not take revenge

--Do not be overcome by evil but overcome evil with good

--If it is possible, as much as it depends on you, live at peace with everyone

Trust in the Lord, and he will direct your path. That path doesn't always appear the same. It is often through green pastures, and sometimes beside still waters. But always it is the path of righteousness. The path of loving our family and loving our enemy is the same path, just a different portion of the trail. Some hikes are easy; others are strenuous. The mountain described above is easier when it is for people we love, when it is summer, and all is green. It becomes more difficult in winter, when the path seems cold and barren. When the reward does not seem worth the risk.

When Jesus told us to "turn the other cheek" it was a tectonic shift in humanity's world view. It is one of the most difficult policies to follow and probably one of the most misunderstood as well. Jesus was not telling us to overlook or accept the enemy's position. It is simply tactical in nature, a different approach to the rules of engagement. Love and forgiveness do not require reconnection. We are not mandated to allow their continued toxic and abusive behavior in our life. It does not mean we do not stand up to the corrupt character they demonstrate toward us and in the lives of those we love. Forgiveness is a modest reminder that they are accountable to God, not to us.

For some, loving their enemy is easier than loving their neighbor. The enemy comes and goes; the neighbor is constantly there. Our foes are easily recognized and usually similar. Neighbors come in great diversity. It is why the disciples asked, "And who is my neighbor?" Loving our enemy can be accomplished with random acts; loving our neighbor is a constant lifestyle. And at times, we will be allowed to go to war with the former, but never with the latter. Loving our enemy puts us between a rock and a hard place, but do not let them win by cowering below. It is a tough climb, but worth it.

A Rock and a Hard Place: Wait on God

It is one thing to be stuck between a rock and hard place, it is quite another to feel those walls closing in. Maybe it is just our imagination, but we feel the rocks getting closer and closer. The path up seems narrower with each step. And like a bad nightmare, the faster we climb the further back we fall. Gravity pulls us down and the ground gives way beneath us. Clouds roll in, the weather turns dark and stormy. Claustrophobia and hypothermia begin to engulf us and panic sets in. There seems to be no escape.

We feel like we are **running out of time** and though our instincts tell us to move faster, our instructions are just the opposite. Wait here! Wait for me! Wait in the car! Wait just a minute! Wait for it! Wait UP!

Few things make us feel more helpless than being stuck. We get stuck in traffic, stuck in a crowded elevator, stuck at the office or at the doctor, stuck in the mud, stuck in routine. The car won't start, we get delayed at the airport, or catch a slow train at the intersection. **And so, we wait!** And this all begins in the womb. We wait nine months to be born; another twelve months to walk, and another twelve months after that to talk. Then we wait another eighteen years before anyone listens to what we are saying. And then we spend a great deal of our lives in waiting rooms, waiting in line, and waiting on other people. We have little tolerance for waiting, but it is a critical component to our faith.

What we really hate about being stuck is our **loss of control**. It is the feeling of helplessness that disturbs us most. We have things to do and places to be. We have a schedule to keep and everything is in place. These unexpected delays wreak havoc on our plans. And it only makes it worse when we can't see the end. It's bad enough that we are only moving 5mph, but the cars are backed up for miles and we can't even see what the problem is. And the sign says, Next Exit in 6 miles.

There is little about faith that brings more conflicting information than the subject of waiting on God. It is impossible to please God without faith, but this part of the climb seems implausible and contradictory. We are told, for instance, to run with patience, but isn't that an oxymoron? We are told to climb and then to be still. Our instructions are to be patient in affliction and to endure hardness. We want to keep moving forward but God tells us to wait. And the worst part, He does not tell us for how long.

Solomon told us that to everything there is a time and a season. And that would be fine if only we were given a calendar of God's timetable. We would like to know if this wait is a short period or an entire season. Is it even going to happen in this calendar year? But Solomon can only offer us this ray of hope: God makes everything beautiful

in its own time. It is poetic and inspirational, one of my favorite verses. It makes perfect sense on top of the mountain, but not when we are climbing on our hands and feet.

What is the purpose of this wait and see game? Why is there not more information forthcoming? We do not care for suspense. Give us some idea; throw us a bone. The crowds implored of Jesus, "When will these things happen?" And all He would tell them was to watch. In the same chapter, Solomon called this waiting room "the burden" because, *"People cannot see the entire scope of God's work."*

It is the prophet Isaiah who gives us the clearest explanation. *"Those who **wait on the Lord** will renew their strength. They will mount up with wings of eagles, they will run and not grow weary, they will walk and not faint."* (40:31)

There it is! The purpose of waiting is for strength conditioning. It is about becoming spiritually fit in areas like patience, tolerance, contentment, and peace. This part of the climb is the steepest with the greatest gravitational pull. We fight and resist it, but that is how strength is built, in the resistance. It is not instant; it comes with time and effort. It is accumulative in its progression.

Simon Peter clearly did not have a "sit and wait" personality. He was definitively not the contemplative type. He was the "shoot first" kind of person, which of course got him into trouble at times. He probably grappled much with the concept of waiting on God. Peter often learned lessons the hard way, but he did learn the lessons. Listen to how he spoke about this necessary piece of faith.

> *"Be humble in the presence of God's mighty power, and he will honor you **when the time comes**. God cares for you, so turn all your worries over to him. Be on your guard and stay awake. Your enemy, the devil, is like a roaring lion, sneaking around to find someone to attack. But you must resist the devil and **stay strong in your faith**. You know that all over the world the Lord's followers are suffering just as you are. But God shows undeserved kindness to everyone. That is why he appointed Christ Jesus to choose you to share in his eternal glory. You will suffer for a while, but God will **make you complete**, steady, strong, and firm. God will be in control forever! Amen."*

Waiting on God is as transparent in the Bible as any other theology. There is even a number that is associated with it—the number 40. It rained 40 days and nights, Israel was 40 years in the wilderness, Jesus fasted 40 days before his temptation in the desert and was here 40 days after the resurrection. The word *quarantine* comes from the Italian language meaning 40 days. This is not the magic number in every situation, rather a systematic way of reminding us that growth does not happen overnight. There is an incubation and it varies in its duration. But it is never **lost or wasted** time. While you are trying to figure it out God has already worked it out.

Now this is crucial to remember! Just because we are waiting does not mean that God is idle. He is at work preparing the road ahead. At times He walks beside us, but when He tells us to, "Wait here," He is walking ahead of us. He is working on the infrastructure, making sure the roads and bridges ahead are safe. We hate seeing construction signs when we travel but they are there for our safety. And the penalties are doubled if we do not slow down and wait. God is surveying and triangulating the new coordinates. He needs to recalibrate every time we get out ahead of Him.

> We plant, we water and then we wait.

Galatians 6:9--Do not grow weary in doing good, for in due season we will reap if we do not faint. (KJV)

Psalm 37:7—Be still before the Lord and wait patiently for Him. (ESV)

Psalm 27:14—Wait for the Lord; be strong and take heart and wait for the Lord. (NIV)

Before we move on, I must confess that this waiting process does not come easy for me. I have never been the type to sit around. There resides in me this constant drive to make something, repair something, finish something. Do something! At the same time, I can say with full assurance that God's timing is always perfect. I say that in retrospect, but hindsight has helped me to grow stronger in foresight. Some of the most meaningful conversations about faith between my wife and me concern God's timing in our lives and marriage. Our faith has grown stronger each time we have waited on Him.

A Rock and a Hard Place: Tame your Tongue

Very often while driving on an interstate you will see litter on the side of the road: bottles, cans, and fast food paper bags. When you are on I-285 bypassing Atlanta you will see appliances, furniture, and mattresses on the shoulder of the road. We have seen washing machines and recliners. How does anyone drive along at 70 mph decide, "Oh, here is a good place to drop off this old refrigerator?" Garbage and trash is being hurled from vehicles, jeopardizing other motorists, and destroying the scenery.

Why do people litter? It's easy, convenient, and self-serving. There is little thought to the harm it causes and to who must clean up the mess. In comparison, we do the same thing with our tongue.

Words matter and we need to be cautious of littering the landscape of the lives of other people with our rubbish. Each item we toss carries a hefty fine and we will give an account of every idle word.

In scripture we are given a detailed list of what this rubbish consists of:

--Do not curse--Do not judge--Do not gossip

--Do not boast--Do not lie--Do not slander

James calls the tongue an "unruly evil" with the destructive power of fire. He was baffled that out of the same mouth of Christ-followers came both blessing and cursing, and he extoled us that this double standard should not exist among true believers. It is why he exhorts us to always be "I." Paul also reminded us to *"Let no unwholesome talk come out of your mouth, but only what builds others UP,"* and to *"let your conversation always be full of grace and seasoned with salt."*

You have often heard the phrase, "He curses like a sailor." I am not sure of the history of why that is so common among that profession. Maybe because they are quarantined in such proximity to other people for long periods of time. When Paul went on his mission journeys he often traveled by ship and ministered in many coastal cities. The language of vulgarity was commonplace. But he also observed that this dialogue continued to be second nature to those who had become Christians. It is fascinating how this "speech littering" is still so widespread among believers today. Often people say, "Don't just talk the talk but walk the walk." However, the opposite should be just as true.

Solomon told us in Proverbs 21 that *"He who keeps his mouth and tongue keeps himself from evil."*

Jesus said to his followers, *"What comes out of the mouth proceeds from the heart, and this defiles a person."* James was so appalled by this behavior that he said, *"Out of the same mouth comes blessing and cursing. These things just should not be!"* Paul was adamant about putting an end to this practice among believers. He told those who lived in the seaport city of Colossi, *"You must put away: anger, wrath, malice, slander, and **obscene talk** from your mouth."*

The most dangerous words that emanate from our lips are what we refer to as "hate speech." It is the language that can devastate individuals and people groups. It reveals itself in prejudice, stereotypes, racism, and discrimination. Sometimes it is blatant, at other times subtle, but its intent is always clear. And I have heard it equally as often from believers as I have non-believers. There is no place for it anywhere, and certainly not from those who truly know God. He speaks the language of love, and kindness, and justice. He created mankind with multiple diversity but zero superiority. ALL nations are blessed in Him and he shows no mercy to the intolerant. Paul said, "There is no Jew, there is no Greek, but all are under his hand." And he admonished us to lead others out of this pit.

This chasm between the rock and hard place of speech is a daily climb. We slip and fall so easily in the loose impediment of sarcastic retort, vulgarity, and name calling. There may be no other area of our lives where it is more important to **go higher, not lower**. To express the lofty courage of grace and not cower to the base of judgement, hate, boasting, and dehumanizing. This language remains all too common for those who claim to follow Christ. There is a time to speak and a time to remain silent. A time to be bold and a time to be humble. We have been given a voice and God demands that we use it to raise consciousness and awareness but not vilify others by our own conscience.

The Philistines had perfected the art of speech bullying. Their initial tactic was always an effort to belittle their opponents into submission. They referred to them as worms, ants, and dogs, an effort to intimidate them. They were giants, they fought from above by talking down to others. It was a battle of wits and it often becomes easy to get caught up in that. The war of words become the thorns, weeds, and poisonous undergrowth during our ascent. The words we choose have the power to raise or the capacity to destroy the human spirit. As Paul said, "To tear down or build up."

These are the rocks and hard places of our faith. Loving our enemies, waiting on God, and taming our tongue are not simply matters of what we cease to do, but what we strive to accomplish. They are opportunities to change destinies. They are not just about forgetting the past they are about climbing to change the future. They are heroic acts of faith and they are highly commendable to God.

Scripture tells us to be tenderhearted and kind to everyone.

Years after David had lost his best friend, Jonathan continued to have an impact on his life. We are told the beautiful story of David helping someone else out of a rock and a hard place.

> *2 Samuel 4:4—"Jonathan, the son of Saul, had a son who was crippled in his feet. He was five years old when the news about Saul and Jonathan came from Jezreel, and his nurse took him up and fled, and as she fled in her haste, he fell and became lame. And his name was Mephibosheth."*

> *2 Samuel 9:1—"And David said, 'Is there still anyone left of the house of Saul, that I may show him kindness for Jonathan's sake?' Ziba said to the king, 'There is still a son of Jonathan; he is crippled in his feet.' And Mephibosheth the son of Jonathan, son of Saul, came to David and fell on his face and paid homage. And David said, 'Mephibosheth!' And he answered, 'Behold, I am your servant.' And David said to him, 'Do not fear, for I will show you kindness for the sake of your father Jonathan, and I will **restore to you all the land of Saul your father, and you shall eat at my table always.**'"*

CHAPTER SEVEN
THE WATCHMEN

The eyes of the Lord are in every place, keeping watch on the evil and the good. - Proverbs 15:3

When Jonathan's war began on the mountaintop, the first to observe the chaos were the watchmen of Saul's army. These guards were tasked with observing enemy movements and advances. But what was taking place above was neither. Their message to the king was baffling; it simply stated that the Philistine army was dispersing. When asked in what direction, they said, "In every direction!" Their job was not to explain it, just report it. The obvious curiosity was how they missed Jonathan and his aide slipping out of the camp? The answer is relatively simple. They were so busy making sure no one snuck in; it never occurred to them that someone might sneak out. Their eyes were fixed on the problem, not the solution. They were defensive players, not part of the offensive unit.

The job description of a watchmen had two major requirements. The first was a heightened awareness of all their senses. This demanded keen eyesight with the ability to recognize every tiny movement. No contacts or cataracts in this workplace. Those on the nightshift must excel in hearing and distinguishing the complex sounds of the dark. These men had to possess an intuition about things that did not feel right. The other quality that was mandatory for this position was unwavering dependability. Those caught sleeping on the job were not fired, they were put to death. Someone must always be watching. That is why they had watchmen, not a watchman.

1 Samuel 14

*And the **watchmen** of Saul in Gibeah of Benjamin looked, and behold, the multitude was dispersing here and there. Then Saul said to the people who were with him, "Count and see who has gone from us." And when they had counted, behold, Jonathan and his armor-bearer were not there.*

Through the years the United States has enacted scores of privacy laws dealing with the regulations of collecting, storing, and using personally identifiable information with regards to family, healthcare, and finances. To enforce these laws, they placed myriad "watchdog" groups to monitor the actions of those who seek to steal this information. Cyber criminals, identity thieves, hackers, and stalkers all move through the dark web of the internet and we depend on the experts to be our watchmen.

Smile, You're on Candid Camera. That catch-phrase was from a television show more than 50 years ago. And at the end of each segment the unwilling participant was pointed to a hidden camera. In today's world the camera is not hidden, and we are routinely aware that someone is always watching. Smile, you are on security camera, I-phone video, dash-cam, intersection recording, doorbell camera, Drone TV, and the satellite network. You are being monitored everywhere you go. Location services can track your movements and provide you with directions. Even your private conversations are overheard, and suggestions then made as to what to buy and where to travel. Our private worlds have been shattered by the overreach of technology. At times we voluntarily surrender this confidence and at other times it is systematically invaded by intruders whom we did not even see coming.

The Privacy of Faith

Jonathan's victory began with a private war within himself. He was a man of faith, but that belief was being tested between a rock and hard place. Namely, between his trust in God and his own personal doubts. For that reason, he told no one about his plan. There was no video recording his movements, no satellites tracking his whereabouts. This was between him and his God. If he died in this pursuit that would be the end of it. Except for the critics who would write about the lunacy and futility of the endeavor. "What was he Thinking?" was what the headline would read. But, if this mission ended in success, the reward would be heralded throughout the countryside and through the annals of history. If he could pull off this incredible feat, then the front page of the newspaper would declare, "God saved Israel Today." But it was not a headline that Jonathan pursued. What he sought was empirical proof that God was capable of accomplishing the impossible. Jonathan's maneuver was timeless and memorable because it began as a private war but ended in vanquishing the enemy and widespread victory for God's kingdom.

Jesus was clear to distinguish the components of our faith that are very private in nature and those that are to be overtly public. Prayer, giving, and fasting should all be done in the secret confines of our relationship with God. In return, God will reward us openly. These elements are deep matters of trust in building our relationship with God, but the results will be keenly observable to the public at large. The portions of our faith that should not be concealed are the courage and devotion to fight for truth and justice. The spread of love, grace, mercy, and kindness are the **philanthropy of real faith**. We should earnestly pray, fast, and give toward these causes but it will be our actions that bring change in the world around us. If there is **no climb** toward these objectives, it brings only disrepute to our faith.

The Pharisees loved to be seen and heard. They wore lavish robes and spoke with many words. They were the embodiment of hypocrisy and Jesus reminded his followers over and over not to be like them. He warned us not to practice our righteousness before people in order to be applauded. If we do, then applause will be our only reward. If we fast only to appear needy, we have not helped the needy. If you sound a trumpet about what you give, then all you have done is paid the piper and have become like a "sounding brass or a tinkling symbol." Jesus said, "You will know them by their fruit," meaning, you will easily recognize them. They are wolves in sheep's clothing. The greatest threats to faith are not the open opponents of it. The **most dangerous existential threats** to Christianity are the hypocrites who pretend to live inside it, those who are more interested in accruing attention than practicing faith.

That behavior is typical for those in the self-employed business of watching. These are the people who have appointed themselves as critics, inspectors, and judges of others. They portend to be the watchmen of truth but are merely attempting to throw light off themselves by disparaging their peers. This is commonly seen in politics but is also deeply seeded in the Church and believers are to be keenly aware of these imposters. They have a form of godliness but deny its power.

Can I help you?

Few usually mean that. You can hear it in the tone of their voice. There is no sincerity behind it. At best it is a hypothetical question and at worst a sarcastic or threatening statement. If an employee asks the question it is normally the result of trained customer service. That is why the call is being recorded for quality assurance. If a stranger asks you that question it is an effort to discover what you are up to. It means "get off my space" or "get out of my face." The inane hypocrisy in the question never solves anything. We know their motive does not align with their query.

One of the very last commands that Jesus gave to his disciples was to **Watch!** He wanted us to be alert to our surroundings as we navigate life between the rock and hard place. The Bible teaches us to **walk by faith**, but it also implores us to **walk in wisdom,** specifically, with those who are outside the faith. We are tasked with the responsibility to serve as the watchmen and guardians of our faith. We are to guard our **hearts and minds.** That is the 18" gap between the rock and hard place; between what we know and what we feel. In our minds we possess wisdom, in our hearts we possess faith.

It is incumbent on us to be **sober and vigilant** because we will be attacked on both fronts simultaneously, the north and south, the flesh and the spirit. The goal of the conflict is not to find peace at the end of the war, but to discover it during the battle. *"The peace of God will guard your **hearts and minds**."*--Philippians 4:7

Get Wisdom!

Solomon is the embodiment of one man's quest for wisdom. In his thirst for learning he discovered that wisdom is a multi-faceted object. It is not one dimensional. More like a prism of light, wisdom is refracted into many colors. Wisdom is inquisitive, it is gained through instruction and formed by knowledge. It seeks to comprehend while at the same time acknowledging that not everything can be understood. It provides us insight and the gift of discernment. It mandates that we show discretion in our choices, and in its most primitive form is simply described as common sense.

There is a trove of important items to pack when preparing for a hike. Necessities like a compass, flashlight, knife, canteen, and first-aid are all critical elements of the backpack. But for me, the one ranking at the top of the list is my hiking stick. For both the ascent and descent this tool provides me the most important weapon I need to fight gravity—**Balance.** The protection afforded most from wisdom is balance. It offers us the ability to both attack and defend and the instincts to know the difference. The rock and hard place is the chasm between grace and truth, the divide between faith and works. **At times we become so a meshed in the theology of our faith that we fail to practice the tenets of our faith.** Solomon gave us example after example of these competing voices—birth/death, plant/reap, love/hate, laugh/cry, gather/let go, war/peace. There are clear and present times for each. And then there is the rock and hard place when they are both present simultaneously.

It is often in those moments when we cry foul! Wait, time out, this is not fair. It may surprise you that the word fair is not in Bible unless it is talking about the weather or someone's complexion. In matters of faith we are not seeking fairness, we are pursuing justice. It is not meaning we are after, but purpose. The "why" question is not for comprehension; it is for action. Rosa Parks was not asking for clarification about why she needed to stand. The "why" for her was motivation for taking a stand.

The Apostle Peter wrote about this in the second chapter of his first book. It is a simple concept to understand but an incredibly difficult assignment to accomplish. He asks us to consider this logic.

"*What credit is it if, when you sin and are beaten for it, you endure? But when you do good and suffer for it and you endure, this is a gracious thing in the sight of God.*" He went on to tell us in chapter three that, "*The eyes of the Lord are always on the righteous. So, it is better to suffer for doing good, if that should be God's will, than for doing evil.*" It is how we respond when no one is watching, except God. These moments do not define you, they refine you.

The most difficult story in the Bible for me to grasp is the enduring tale of Abraham and Isaac. The father is told to sacrifice his son. Yes, I understand the big picture, the symbolism of God offering his only son. But I am sorry; I would have failed that test miserably. We have known far too many friends who have lost children to cancer, car accidents, spider bites, and other tragedies. I cannot imagine anything more difficult in life. I admit there are mysteries too deep for me to fathom, far beyond my understanding, answers that I will never find in this life, mountains that I hope never to be asked to climb. Faith is not an answer to the why question; it is the substance of what we hope for next.

"You will keep the mind that is dependent on you in perfect peace, for it is trusting in you." --Isaiah 26:3

The New Normal

This is the current catch phrase in our society as we begin to move out from under this pandemic. What will life look like in the next few weeks, months, and even years? There are currently more questions than answers. We are residing right now in the "watch" mode. Watching the curve, the statistics, the news, the reactions, the responses, and the results of people attempting to get back to normal. But in the back of our minds, we know that our normal will never look the same. But then, it has always worked that way. In my lifetime alone there have been dozens and dozens of **new normals**. And, the vast majority of the time, the new normal was much better.

Remember also, that it was for this very reason that Jesus said, **"Do not fret."** It is not a commonly used word anymore. It means that we should not agonize about the future. This is a much deeper connotation than the word worry. Anxiety most often leads us to be fearful about something we think will be bad. When we fret, we allow stress to bring agony, a measure of pain amidst the uncertainty. The new normal involves change, and people tend to agonize about change. They have become accustomed to this way of life. It may not be the best, but it seems safer, and is certainly familiar.

Faith always brings us to a new normal. But every time, without exception, it is a better place. We are stronger, richer, and more vibrant about who we are and what we are doing. It has become one of the most trite expressions of our time but none-the-less meaningful: No risk, no reward. Without faith it is impossible to get to the next mountain, the next valley, the next summit. We must stretch it, expand it, and constantly challenge it. The greatest enemy to faith is not fear and doubt, it is comfort and ease.

Normal is simply the time we are waiting on God for the new thing, the next thing. It was the Psalmist who wrote, "*God is always doing a new thing.*"

Get out of your own way

Jonathan was skilled in the tradecraft of archery and God would use this gift to achieve victory. But Jonathan knew that his talent alone would not be enough. He had heard the stories of Abraham, Moses, Joshua, and Samson, but he did not want to live his faith vicariously through them. He wasn't asking God to part a sea, knock down walls, or kill 1,000 men with the jawbone of an ass. But he remembered what Joshua had written immediately following the death of Moses as Israel was about to enter the promise land. *"What I have commanded you today **is not too hard for you,** neither is it far off. My Word is very near to you; it is in your mouth and in your heart, so that **you can do it.**"* Jonathan wanted only to accomplish the task assigned to him; to face a small garrison on top of a hill. To claim his own miracle or seal his own fate, by life or by death.

After Paul completed the eleventh chapter of Hebrews, he followed it immediately with a personal challenge to every believer. *"Since we are surrounded by this great cloud of witnesses, let us also lay aside every weight, and the sin which clings so closely, and let us run with endurance the race that is set **before us.**"* Perhaps motivated by the individual testimonials he had just recounted, the Apostle now wants to make their history relevant. To look at these unsung heroes of faith and examine the **'Why?**

What motivated them? Their stories were all unique, but the Why was always universal. Paul wanted to make certain that each of us have our own race to run and have the capacity to complete the contest. We cannot run someone else's race or compete for their purpose. Paul reminded us of that in his own epitaph. *"I have fought a good fight, I have **finished my course**, I have kept the faith."*

Jonathan was ultimately seeking the answer to his life's greatest dilemma: was faith real? The 'Perhaps' in his mind was not questioning God, it was questioning himself. Have I understood it correctly? He felt like a trial lawyer whose case might be invalid. He had a theory, but it was an untested hypothesis. He had an idea, a belief, but no corroborating evidence. He had motive, but no demonstrable proof. His faith was filled with subjective analysis but not objective facts. There was nothing in his belief system that a judge or jury would find a verdict for. If he were to find the "smoking gun," an excision would have to take place. He needed to cut out the tumors of doubt and fear, to exercise his own demons. So, when the prosecution said, "Come up to us," Jonathan saw his opportunity to crack the case wide open, to adjudicate his faith. He glanced at his assistant and said, "**All right then, let's climb!**"

The Why changes history. The Why changes your history. You can remain hiding under the rocks asking why this happened, or you can use the Why as motivation to rise. To say, "I am tired, not physically tired, just tired of giving in." To begin the Climb of faith and see what is at the pinnacle. To find out if--perhaps—God will fight for me. And to discover, like Jonathan, that...

> The faith to move mountains often requires the courage to CLIMB them

EPILOGUE
ALL RISE

"Many things in life will catch your attention, only a few will grab your heart. Pursue those!" —Michael Nolan

My oldest daughter and I are movie buffs. We used to love going to the theater and afterwards breaking down every aspect and meaning to the movie. On television we enjoyed watching the old classics—Mr. Smith goes to Washington, Citizen Cane, The Grapes of Wrath, and It's a Wonderful Life. Our favorite was To Kill a Mockingbird. So, when it came to Broadway last year, we filled a bucket list item and went to the Schubert Theater in NYC to see

Jeff Daniels portray Atticus Finch. The cast was amazing and the play outstanding, a memorable Father/Daughter date. We laughed and we cried throughout the performance. And then came the most dramatic part of the story. The final two words of the final act. They are uttered by Scout, the daughter of the principled attorney. They not only provide the perfect punctuation to the play itself; they resonate throughout our culture and challenge us to consider our own humanity. They demand us to climb! **"ALL RISE!"**

During the time I was working on this chapter we heard the tragic news about the death of Kobe Bryant and his daughter. While thousands mourned, many posted items and tweets about things they remembered about the basketball legend. One of the most common tributes had to do with his work ethic and perseverance. When I saw this quote, it seemed quite appropriate to include here.

> *"Everything negative—pressure, challenges—it's all an opportunity for me to rise."* --**Kobe Bryant**

Elevation requires Separation

Growth often means that we must leave something behind. It might be people, a job, a habit, or a location. In any event, it is usually something we found comfort and security in, even if it was under a rock in a desert. **To keep your faith advancing, God will remove you from the familiar.** It may feel like you are outnumbered and out maneuvered but that is only because your eyes have not yet been opened. So, let me ask you these questions:

1. What was the greatest act of faith you ever trusted God for?

2. What were the most difficult aspects of that climb?

3. What was your WHY?

4. Who were your armor-bearers?

When Solomon sat down to write the book of Ecclesiastes it began as an attempt to answer the **Why?** The wisdom he had amassed could still not satisfy his deepest concerns of life. So, he began a conversation, first with himself and then with his Creator. We can see his frustration in his inability to make sense of certain aspects of life and we empathize with his agony. The question of the ages is Why? And as Philip Yancey wrote in his book title, it is *The Question that Never Goes Away*.

It is easy to get lost in Solomon's dilemma, to become disoriented and disillusioned. But one of the things we may fail to recognize in his search was that he had discovered certain truths that served as directional points. There are white and blue blazes along the path of faith that provide the certainty we are still moving in the right direction. We may not know what lies ahead, but we can trust the compass.

God's ways are mysterious, but He is not. He doesn't keep his identity a cosmic secret. He doesn't leave clues and riddles. The problem with most seekers is that they are searching for What, not Who. He is in complete control of our ecosystem and he has NEVER relegated that responsibility to anyone.

He doesn't need a dictionary, encyclopedia, or Google. He knows biology, geology, psychology, zoology, physiology, and all the other "ologies." Not a single bird falls to the ground without him being aware of it.

Wisdom may not always provide the answers, but it can always accommodate perspective. That is why Solomon began the last chapter and conclusion to his search with the word, **Remember.** Do not forget where you came from or where you are ultimately going. And as you **climb**, remember two pieces of advice that Solomon left us with.

Chapter 5—*"Don't just dream the dream; work at it."*

Chapter 9—*"Whatever your hand finds to do, do it with all your might."*

Your climb will be filled with unknowns and you will remember all the obstacles that stood in your way. Every rock, thorn, snake, cut, and bruise will leave an indelible mark on your soul. You will not forget the faces of every enemy that hurled insults and threw rocks from above. The shouts that attempt to disregard and diminish your faith will echo for years. But the scars and voices will only serve to acknowledge that you completed the climb. And you **put to flight** the fears, and hate, and critics who opposed you. And these reminders will embolden your resolve to strengthen your faith. And this will be **very pleasing to God.**

In the conclusion to his poetic description of love in I Corinthians 13, Paul wrote that three things will abide in us, no matter the circumstances: Faith, Hope, and Love. **Faith** is the substance of things **hoped** for, **love** is the evidence of what we see. That is why love is the greatest of the three; there is tangible proof of its existence. The first two are not eternal; at some point we will no longer require them. Faith and hope are conditional, love is not. The first two will escape us at times, and we may falter along the climb, but love never fails.

Jesus climbed up, at times on His hands and feet. And like Jonathan's armor bearer, He carried our load. He bore our sin and guilt and shame and delivered it to the pinnacle to defeat the enemy. Sorely outnumbered, He chose not to call his legions of armies. His untimely death sent fear and uncertainty throughout His followers. After His resurrection He found them hiding in the shadows and under the rocks. And when they watched Him arise and ascend back to heaven, they were emboldened with the thing they lacked most when Christ was with them: Faith. The reformation was about to begin, the church about to be born. And so, they began **The Climb.**

Please allow me to leave you with two things that have been instrumental in my personal climb of faith. They are my favorite quote and favorite passage of scripture. They have served as white blazes for me along the path of my own faith. Maybe they will help you along yours.

> *"A ship is safe in the harbor but that is not what it was made for." –John A. Shedd*

> *"Who can separate us from the love of Christ? Can affliction or distress or persecution or famine or nakedness or danger or sword? No, in all these things we are **more than conquerors**, through Him who loved us. For I am persuaded that neither death nor life, nor angels nor rulers, nor things present nor things to come, nor powers, nor height nor depth, nor any other created thing will be able to separate us from the love of God that in in Christ Jesus our Lord." –The Apostle Paul (Romans 8-CSB)*

Now I will leave you exactly where we began. **Without Faith it is Impossible to Please God**

www.ingramcontent.com/pod-product-compliance
Lightning Source LLC
Chambersburg PA
CBHW070158100426
42743CB00013B/2963